Real-Life English

A COMPETENCY–BASED ESL PROGRAM FOR ADULTS

Program Consultants

Jayme Adelson-Goldstein
North Hollywood Learning Center
North Hollywood, California

Julia Collins
Los Angeles Unified School District
El Monte-Rosemead Adult School
El Monte, California

Else V. Hamayan
Illinois Resource Center
Des Plaines, Illinois

Kent Heitman
Carver Community Middle School
Delray Beach, Florida

Patricia De Hesus-Lopez
Texas A & M University
Kingsville, Texas

Federico Salas-Isnardi
Houston Community College
Adult Literacy Programs
Houston, Texas

Connie Villaruel
El Monte-Rosemead Adult School
El Monte, California

Wei-hua (Wendy) Wen
Adult & Continuing Education
New York City Board of Education
New York, New York

STECK-VAUGHN
ELEMENTARY · SECONDARY · ADULT · LIBRARY

A Harcourt Company

www.steck-vaughn.com

ACKNOWLEDGMENTS

Staff Credits:

Executive Editor	♦	Ellen Lehrburger
Senior Editor	♦	Tim Collins
Design Manager	♦	Richard Balsam
Cover Design	♦	Richard Balsam
Photo Editor	♦	Margie Foster

Photo Credits:
Cover: © Randal Alhadeff, Cooke Photographics (title); © Randal Alhadeff–p.2, 3;
© John Charley–p.86, 87; © Gary Christopher–p.30, 31d; Bob Daemmrich–p.11a, 11b,
11f, 11g, 11i, 12a, 12b, 12f, 12g, 12i, 31a; © Jack Demuth–p.73a, 101c, 101d, 118, 126;
© Patti Gilliam–p.13, 116, 125, 128, 129; © Stephanie Huebinger–p.4, 44; © John Langford–p.46;
Phyllis Liedecker–p.11c, 11d, 11e, 11h, 12c, 12d, 12e, 12h, 16, 17, 59, 117;
Joan Menschefreund–p.45c; © Daniel Thompson Photography–p.6, 27, 49, 51, 53, 54, 58, 72,
73b, 74, 88, 100, 101a, 101b, 109, 110; © Mary Pat Waldron–p.114, 115.

Additional Photography by:
P.31b William Birdsong/Georgia State Photographer; p.31c Supreme Court
Historical Society; p.33a White House Photos; p.33b Supreme Court Historical Society;
p.33c William Birdsong/Georgia State Photographer; p.45a Montauk Pt. State Park, NY;
p.45b Colorado Department of Public Relations; p.45d © Fernando Bueno/The Image Bank;
p.48a © Churchill & Klehr/Tony Stone Worldwide; p.48b © Tony Stone Worldwide;
p.48c © Paul Nehrenz/The Image Bank; p.56 © D. Donne Bryant Stock Photography.

Illustration Credits:
The Ivy League of Artists, Inc.

Additional Illustration by:
Scott Bieser–p.88, 85; Tami Crabb–p.117d; David Griffin–p.93.

Contributing Writer to the First Edition:
Lynne Lilley Robinson
Division of Adult and Continuing Education
Sweetwater Union High School District, Chula Vista, California

Electronic Production:
International Electronic Publishing Center, Inc.

CONTENTS

Real-Life English is a complete competency-based, four-skill program for teaching ESL to adults and young adults. *Real-Life English* follows a competency-based syllabus that is compatible with the CASAS and MELT (BEST Test) competencies, as well as state curriculums for competency-based adult ESL from Texas and California.

Real-Life English is designed for students enrolled in public or private schools, in learning centers, or in institutes, and for individuals working with tutors. The program consists of four levels plus a Literacy Level for use prior to or together with Level 1. *Real-Life English* has these components:

◆ Five Student Books (Literacy and Levels 1–4).

◆ Five Teacher's Editions (Literacy and Levels 1–4), which provide detailed suggestions on how to present each section of the Student Book in class.

◆ Four Workbooks (Levels 1–4), which provide reinforcement for each section of the Student Books.

◆ Audiocassettes (Literacy and Levels 1–4), which contain all dialogs and listening activities in the Student Books. This symbol on the Student Book page indicates each time material for that page is on the Audiocassettes. A transcript of all material recorded on the tapes but not appearing directly on the Student Book pages is at the back of each Student Book and Teacher's Edition.

Each level consists of ten units. Because the unit topics carry over from level to level, *Real-Life English* is ideal for multi-level classes.

 The *About You* symbol, a unique feature, appears on the Student Book page each time students use a competency. To facilitate personalization, color is used in dialogs and exercises. After students have learned a dialog or completed an exercise, they can easily adapt it to talk or write about themselves by changing the words in color.

Organization of Student Book 2

Each unit contains these eleven sections:

Unit Opener

Each Unit Opener includes a list of unit competencies, a photo and accompanying questions, and a dialog, a brief story, or a short article. (In Level 1 only, a chant always appears on this page.) Teachers can use the list of competencies for their own reference, or they can have students read it so that they, too, are aware of the unit's goals. The photo and questions activate students' prior knowledge by getting them to think and talk about the unit topic. The dialog, article, or story gets students reading, thinking, and talking about the unit topic.

Starting Out

Starting Out presents most of the new competencies, concepts, and language in the unit. It generally consists of a dialog or captioned pictures, questions, and an *About You* activity.

Talk It Over

Talk It Over introduces additional competencies, language, and concepts, usually in the form of a dialog. The dialog becomes the model for an interactive *About You* activity.

Word Bank

Word Bank presents and develops vocabulary. The first part of the page contains a list of the new key words and phrases grouped by category. The Useful Language box contains common expressions, clarification strategies, and idioms students use in the unit. Oral and written exercises and *About You* activities provide purposeful and communicative reinforcement of the new vocabulary.

Listening

The Listening page develops competency-based listening comprehension skills. Tasks include listening for supervisors' instructions at work, prices and totals, directions, and doctors' instructions.

All the activities develop the skill of **focused listening.** Students learn to recognize the information they need and listen selectively for only that information. They do not have to understand every word; rather, they have to filter out everything except the information they want to find out. This essential skill is used by native speakers of all languages.

Many of the activities involve **multi-task listening.** Students listen to the same selection several times and complete a different task each time. First they might listen for the main idea. They might listen again for specific information. They might listen a third time in order to draw conclusions or make inferences.

Culminating discussion questions allow students to relate the information they have heard to their own needs and interests.

Reading

The selections in Reading, such as food package directions, rental ads, and articles on bank services and effective job interviewing techniques, focus on life-skill based tasks. Exercises, discussion questions, and *About You* activities develop reading skills and help students relate the content of the selections to their lives.

Structure Base

Structure Base, a two-page spread, presents key grammatical structures that complement the unit competencies. Language boxes show the new language in a clear, simple format that allows students to make generalizations about the new language. Oral and written exercises provide contextualized reinforcement of each new grammar point.

Writing

On the Writing page students develop authentic writing skills, such as filling out bank forms, completing citizenship applications, writing shopping lists, and completing medical history forms.

One To One

Each One To One section presents a competency-based information-gap activity. Students are presented with incomplete or partial information that they must complete by finding out the missing information from their partners. Topics include returning articles to a store, applying for jobs, reading rental ads, and comparing sales at two stores. In many units, culminating discussion questions encourage students to relate the information they gathered to their own needs and interests.

Extension

The Extension page enriches the previous instruction with activities at a slightly more advanced level. As in other sections, realia is used extensively. Oral and written exercises and *About You* activities help students master the competencies, language, and concepts, and relate them to their lives.

Check Your Competency

The Check Your Competency pages are designed to allow teachers to track students' progress and to meet schools' or programs' learner verification needs. All competencies are tested in the same manner they are presented in the units, so formats are familiar and non-threatening, and success is built in. The list of competencies at the top of the page alerts teachers and students to the competencies that are being evaluated. The check-off boxes allow students to track their success and gain a sense of accomplishment and satisfaction.

 This *Check Up* symbol on the Check Your Competency pages denotes when a competency is evaluated. For more information on this section, see "Evaluation" on page viii.

Placement

Any number of tests can be used to place students in the appropriate level of *Real-Life English.* The following tables indicate placement based on the CASAS and MELT (BEST Test) standards.

Student Performance Levels	CASAS Achievement Score	Real-Life English
	164 or under	Literacy
I	165–185	Level 1
II	186–190	
III	191–196	Level 2
IV	197–205	
V	206–210	Level 3
VI	211–216	
VII	217–225	Level 4
VIII	226 (+)	

Teaching Techniques

Presenting Dialogs

To present a dialog, follow these suggestions:

♦ Play the tape or say the dialog aloud two or more times. Ask one or two simple questions to make sure students understand.

♦ Say the dialog aloud line-by-line for students to repeat chorally, by rows, and then individually.

♦ Have students say or read the dialog together in pairs.

♦ Have several pairs say or read the dialog aloud for the class.

Presenting Articles

To present the brief articles in the Unit Openers, follow these steps:

♦ Have students use the photograph and the unit title to make predictions about what the article might be about. Restate the students' ideas and/or write them on the board in acceptable English.

♦ Play the tape or read the article aloud as students follow along in their books.

♦ Ask a few simple questions to make sure that students understand the main ideas. Have students refer to the predictions written on the board. Ask them to say which of the predictions are correct.

♦ Have them read the article again independently.

♦ Discuss the article with students. Ask additional comprehension questions. You might also ask the class to summarize the article, to state their opinions about it, or to state whether they agree with everything in the article.

Presenting Stories

To present the brief stories in the Unit Opener, follow these steps.

♦ Have students use the photograph and the unit title to make inferences about what the story might be about. Have them scan the story for the names of the characters. Have students talk about what the relationship among the people might be and what the story might say about them. Write their ideas on the board or restate them in acceptable English.

♦ Play the tape or read the story aloud as students follow along in their books.

♦ Ask a few simple questions to make sure that students understand the main ideas. Have students refer to the predictions written on the board. Ask them to say which of them are correct.

♦ Have them read the story again independently.

♦ Discuss the story with students. Ask additional comprehension questions. You might also ask students to summarize the story or to say if they or anyone they know has had experiences similar to the ones in the story.

Reinforcing Vocabulary

To reinforce the words in the list on the Word Bank page, have students look over the list. Clarify any words they do not recognize. To provide additional reinforcement, use any of these techniques:

♦ **Vocabulary notebooks.** Have students use each new word to say a sentence for you to write on the board. Have students copy all of the sentences into their vocabulary notebooks.

♦ **Personal dictionaries.** Students can start personal dictionaries. For each new word students can write a simple definition and/or draw or glue in a picture of the object or the action.

♦ **Flash cards.** Flash cards are easy for you or for students to make. Write a new word or phrase on the front of each card. Provide a simple definition or a picture of the object or action on the back of the card. Students can use the cards to review vocabulary or to play a variety of games, such as Concentration.

♦ **The Remember-It Game.** Use this simple memory game to review vocabulary of every topic. For example, to reinforce food words, start the game by saying, *We're having a picnic, and we're going to bring apples.* The next student has to repeat the list and add an item. If someone cannot remember the whole list or cannot add a word, he or she has to drop out. The student who can remember the longest list wins.

Presenting Listening Activities

Use any of these suggestions:

♦ To activate students' prior knowledge, have them look at the illustrations, if any, and say as much as they can about them. Encourage them to make inferences about the content of the listening selection.

♦ Have students read the directions. To encourage them to focus their listening, have them read the questions so that they know exactly what to listen for.

♦ Play the tape or read the Listening Transcript aloud as students complete the activity. Rewind the tape and play it again as necessary.

♦ Check students' work.

In multi-task listenings, remind students that they will listen to the same passage several times and answer different questions each time. After students complete a section, check their work (or have students check their own or each others' work) before you rewind the tape and proceed to the next section.

Prereading

To help students read the selections with ease and success, establish a purpose for reading and call on students' prior knowledge to make inferences about the reading. Use any of these techniques:

♦ Have students look over and describe any photographs, realia, and/or illustrations. Ask them to use the illustrations to say what they think the selection might be about.

♦ Have students read the title and any heads or sub-heads. Ask them what kind of information they think is in the selection and how it might be organized. Ask them where they might encounter such information outside of class and why they would want to read it.

♦ Have students read the questions that follow the selection to help them focus their reading. Ask them what kind of information they think they will find out when they read. Restate their ideas and/or write them on the board in acceptable English.

♦ Remind students that they do not have to know all the words in order to understand the selection. Then have students complete the activities on the page. Check their answers.

One To One

To use these information gap activities to maximum advantage, follow these steps:

- Put students in pairs, assign the roles of A and B, and have students turn to the appropriate pages. Make sure that students look only at their assigned pages.

- Present the dialog in Step 1. Follow the instructions in "Presenting Dialogs" on page vi. (Please note that as these conversations are intended to be models for free conversation, they are not recorded on the Audiocassettes.)

- When students can say the dialog with confidence, model Step 2 with a student. Remind students that they need to change the words in color to adapt the dialog in 1 to each new situation. Then have students complete the activity.

- Have students continue with the remaining steps on the page. For additional practice, make sure students switch roles (Student A becomes Student B and vice versa) and repeat Steps 2 and 3. When all students have completed all parts of both pages, check everyone's work, or have students check their own or each others' work.

Evaluation

To use the Check Your Competency pages successfully, follow these suggested procedures.

Before and during each evaluation, create a relaxed, affirming atmosphere. Chat with the students for a few minutes and review the material. When you and the students are ready, have students read the directions and look over each exercise before they complete it. If at any time you sense that students are becoming frustrated, stop to provide additional review. Resume when students are ready. The evaluation formats follow two basic patterns:

1. Speaking competencies are checked in the same two-part format used to present them in the unit. In the first part, a review, students fill in missing words in a brief conversation. In the second part, marked with the *Check Up*

symbol, students' ability to use the competency is checked. Students use the dialog they have just completed as a model for their own conversations. As in the rest of the unit, color indicates the words students change to talk about themselves. Follow these suggestions:

- When students are ready, have them complete the written portion. Check their answers. Then have students practice the dialog in pairs.

- Continue with the spoken part of the evaluation. Make sure that students remember that they are to substitute words about themselves for the words in color. Have students complete the spoken part in any or all of these ways:

Self- and Peer Evaluation: Have students complete the spoken activity in pairs. Students in each pair evaluate themselves and/or each other and report the results to you.

Teacher/Pair Evaluation: Have pairs complete the activity as you observe. Begin with the most proficient students. As other students who are ready to be evaluated wait, have them practice in pairs. Students who complete the evaluation successfully can peer-teach those who are waiting or those who need additional review.

Teacher/Individual Evaluation: Have individuals complete the activity with you as partner. Follow the procedures in Teacher/Pair Evaluation.

2. Listening, reading, and **writing** competencies are checked in a simple one-step process. When students are ready to begin, have them read the instructions. Demonstrate the first item and have students complete the activity. Then check their work. If necessary, provide any review needed, and have students try the activity again.

When students demonstrate mastery of a competency to your satisfaction, have them record their success by checking the appropriate box at the top of their Student Book page. The Teacher's Edition also contains charts for you to reproduce and use to keep track of individual and class progress.

Real-Life English

Personal Communication

Unit Competencies

1. Identify people in your family
2. Give personal information
3. Introduce people
4. Describe people
5. Apply for a driver's license

What's she doing? What's she saying? What do you think?

Alberto called Ji Sun last week. Practice the dialog.

➤ Hi, Ji Sun. How's it going?

● Pretty good, Alberto. What's new?

➤ Not much. Do you want to go to a movie tonight?

● I can't. It's my grandmother's birthday.

➤ How old is she?

● Seventy-five.

➤ Wow! Does she live in the U.S. now?

● No. She's only visiting.

➤ Well, "Happy birthday" to her.

Starting Out

 A. Today Ji Sun is showing Alberto some pictures of her family. Look and read.

1. My mother and father and I
    live together.
   My brother, Lin, doesn't live
    with us.
   He lives in Los Angeles.
   He has brown eyes
    and black hair.
   He's very tall and thin.

2. Uncle Lu and Aunt Mary
    live near us.
   Their son, Allen, is my cousin.
   My grandfather and grandmother
    Park are visiting them.
   My grandparents live in Korea.
   They speak Korean.
   They speak very little English.

B. Answer the questions.

1. How many people are in Ji Sun's family?
2. What's her family like?

 C. Work with a partner.
   Use sentences like the ones in A to talk about your family.

Talk It Over

 A. In most states people can get driver's licenses when they're 16 years old. Marge is applying for a license. Practice the dialog.

➤ Here's my driver's license application.
● Let's see. . . . Oh, you didn't answer a few questions. What color is your hair?
➤ **Blond.**
● And your eyes?
➤ **Blue.**
● Do you wear glasses?
➤ **No.**
● How old are you?
➤ I'm **35.**
● Are you married or single?
➤ I'm **divorced, actually.**
● Oh, OK. Now you can take the written test.

B. Talk to other students. Complete the sentences. Write the students' names on the lines.

1. <u>Marge</u> has blue eyes.

2. _____ has a birthday this month.

3. _____ isn't married.

4. _____ is an aunt.

5. _____ wears glasses.

4   Unit 1

Word Bank

A. Study the vocabulary.

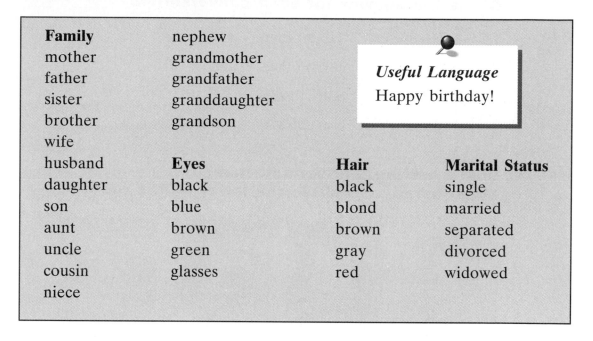

Family
mother
father
sister
brother
wife
husband
daughter
son
aunt
uncle
cousin
niece

nephew
grandmother
grandfather
granddaughter
grandson

Useful Language
Happy birthday!

Eyes	**Hair**	**Marital Status**
black	black	single
blue	blond	married
brown	brown	separated
green	gray	divorced
glasses	red	widowed

B. Use the family tree to complete the sentences.

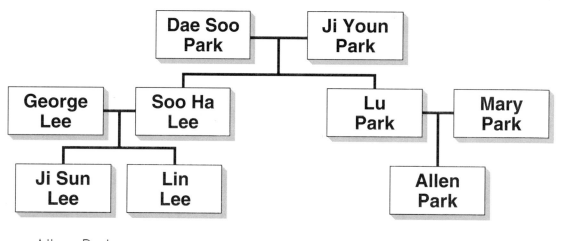

1. <u>Allen Park</u> **(Allen Park/Mary Park)** is Ji Sun's cousin.

2. Lin Lee is Ji Sun's _____ **(uncle/brother)**.

3. _____ **(Lu Park/George Lee)** is Ji Sun's uncle.

4. George Lee is Ji Sun's _____ **(sister/father)**.

C. Make a family tree for your family on a sheet of paper. Write their names on the tree.

Listening

A. Look and listen. Who does Lucy introduce to Duc?
Circle the answer for each conversation.

1. (her mother)   her brother

2. her father   her brother

3. her uncle   her cousin

4. her sister   her uncle

B. Who's getting a driver's license?
Look, listen, and circle the letter of the picture.

a.

b.

c.

d.

e.

Listen again.
Complete the driver's license application for Sang Qun Thin.

DRIVER'S LICENSE APPLICATION

Last Name	First Name			
Thin	Sang Qun			

ADDRESS NUMBER AND STREET	BIRTH DATE		
	MONTH	DAY	YEAR
	4	12	68

CITY Miami	STATE	ZIP CODE

EYE COLOR	SEX Male	HEIGHT 5 Feet 3 Inches	WEIGHT	HAIR COLOR

PLACE OF BIRTH , Korea	PHONE

Reading

A. Look and read.

Pictures of children in the U.S. who are lost or missing sometimes appear on milk cartons. Read about these missing children.

Have you seen me?
Name: Luis Garcia
Age: 8
Weight: 55 pounds
Height: 4 feet 2 inches
Hair: Black
Eyes: Brown
Sex: Male

Have you seen me?
Name: Carol Mayer
Age: 13
Weight: 90 pounds
Height: 4 feet 11 inches
Hair: Blond
Eyes: Blue
Sex: Female

B. Answer the questions about Luis and Carol.

_____c_____   1. How much does Carol weigh?   a. black

_____   2. How tall is Luis?   b. blue

_____   3. What color are Carol's eyes?   ✔ c. 90 pounds

_____   4. What color is Luis's hair?   d. 4 feet 2 inches

C. Answer the questions.

1. Why do you think the children are lost?
2. Have you ever heard about a lost child?

Structure Base

A. Study the examples.

I'm	tall.
He's	
She's	

We're	tall.
You're	
They're	

B. Complete the sentences. Use the words from A.

1. My name's Ana. _____I'm_____ tall and thin.

2. My son's name is Rico. _____ thin, too. _____
   not very tall.

3. Rico's like my parents. _____ not very tall, either.

C. Study the examples.

I	live in an apartment.
We	
You	
They	

| He | lives in an apartment. |
| She | |

D. Complete the passage. Write the correct word form.

My friend **Ivan** _____speaks_____ (speak) **English** and **Russian**.

His mother's name is **Anna**. **His** father's name is **Misha**.

They're from **Russia**. Now they _____ (live) in **the U.S.**

His mother _____ (speak) **English** and **Russian**.

His father _____ (speak) only **Russian**.

**E. Work with a partner. Use the sentences in D.
Talk about your family or your friends.**

F. Study the examples.

I We You They	have brown hair.

He She	has brown hair.

G. Complete the sentences. Use the words from F.

1. I _____have_____ **brown** hair and **brown** eyes.

2. My friend **Mei** _____ **black** hair and **brown** eyes.

3. My friends **Ana** and **Ed** _____ **blond** hair and **blue** eyes.

4. Our teacher _____ **red** hair and **green** eyes.

H. Work with a partner.
Use the sentences in G to talk about people in your class.

I. Study the examples.

I	me
he	him
she	her
we	us
you	you
they	them

My grandparents are visiting us.

J. Complete the sentences. Use the words from I.

1. You should meet **Elena.**   You should meet ___her___.

2. I'd like to meet **Marco and Rosa.**   I'd like to meet _____.

3. I'm meeting Rico's **uncle.**   I'm meeting _____.

4. Please introduce **Alicia and me.**   Please introduce _____.

Write It Down

**A. Look at the picture.
Read the application.**

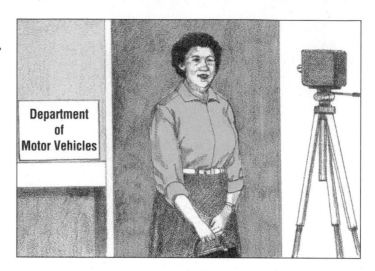

Department
of
Motor Vehicles

DRIVER'S LICENSE APPLICATION

NAME		
Last	First	Middle
Stark	Rita	Arlene

ADDRESS		
Number and Street		
321 North Spruce Street		

CITY	STATE	ZIP CODE
Chicago	Illinois	60022

BIRTH DATE			SEX	HEIGHT	WEIGHT
MONTH	DAY	YEAR	female	5 feet 6 inches	168 pounds
6	10	34	HAIR COLOR black	EYE COLOR brown	

About
You

**B. Complete the application.
Write about yourself.**

DRIVER'S LICENSE APPLICATION

NAME		
Last	First	Middle

ADDRESS		
Number and Street		

CITY	STATE	ZIP CODE

BIRTH DATE			SEX	HEIGHT	WEIGHT
MONTH	DAY	YEAR			
			HAIR COLOR	EYE COLOR	

I. Practice the dialog.

➤ Who's **Eva Tena's son?**

● His name is **Rolando Tena.**

➤ How do you spell that?

● **His** first name is **Rolando, R-O-L-A-N-D-O.**
  His last name is **Tena, T-E-N-A.**

Rosa
Tena

Mario
Reyna

Elena
Reyna

Rita
Tena

Oscar
Tena

Eva
Tena

Rolando
Tena

About
You

2. What are their names? Use the dialog in I to ask Student B. Write the information on the family tree.

Who's Eva Tena's son?
Who's Rolando Tena's uncle?
Who's Oscar Tena's father?

About
You

3. What are their names? Use the dialog in I to tell Student B.

4. Switch roles. Turn to page 12. Complete 2 and 3.

One To One

Student B

I. Practice the dialog.

➤ Who's **Eva Tena's son?**

● His name is **Rolando Tena.**

➤ How do you spell that?

● **His** first name is **Rolando, R-O-L-A-N-D-O.**
His last name is **Tena, T-E-N-A.**

Pablo
Tena

_____

_____ _____

Elena
Reyna

_____
_____

Oscar
Tena

Eva
Tena

Carlos
Reyna

Rolando
Tena

2. What are their names? Use the dialog in I to tell Student A.

3. What are their names? Use the dialog in I to ask Student A. Write the information on the family tree.

Who's Oscar Tena's mother?
Who's Pablo Tena's daughter?
Who's Eva Tena's father?

4. Switch roles. Turn to page II. Complete 2 and 3.

12

Unit 1

Extension

 A. Practice the dialog.

> ➤ Good morning, **Soo Ha.**
> ● Good morning, **Ms. Mendoza.**
>   I'd like you to meet **Bill Perry.**
>   **He's a new salesperson.**
> ➤ Nice to meet you, **Bill.**
>   We're glad to have you here.
> ■ Thank you, **Ms. Mendoza.**
>   It's nice to meet you, too.

 B. Work with two students.
Use the dialog in A to introduce yourselves.

 C. Practice the dialog.

> ➤ Hi! Are you **the new employee?**
> ■ Yes. I'm **Bill Perry.**
> ➤ **Bill,** it's good to meet you.
>   I'm **Paco Gonzales.**
> ■ Sorry, what was your name again?
> ➤ **Paco Gonzales.**
> ■ Good to meet you, **Paco.**
> ➤ Good to meet you, too, **Bill.**
>   I'll see you around.

 D. Work with a partner.
Use the dialog in C to introduce yourselves.

Can you use the competencies?

- [ ] 1. Identify people in your family
- [ ] 2. Give personal information
- [ ] 3. Introduce people
- [ ] 4. Describe people
- [ ] 5. Apply for a driver's license

A. Review competency I. Complete the dialog.

| name   sisters |

➤ What's your mother's _____?
● Her name's **Margarita Coto.**

➤ Do you have brothers or _____?
● **Yes. I have five sisters.**

**Use competency I.
Use the dialog above to talk about your family or friends.**

B. Review competency 2. Complete the dialog.

✔

| married   name   old |

➤ What's your _____*name*_____?
● **Ellen Thompson.**

➤ How _____ are you?
● I'm **33.**

➤ Are you _____?
● **Yes, I am.**

**Use competency 2.
Use the dialog above to talk about yourself.**

C. Review competency 3.
Complete the dialog.

✔

meet you nice

➤ Hi, **Franco.** I want you to _____meet_____ my cousin, Blanca.

● Hi, **Blanca.** Nice to meet _____.

■ _____ to meet you, too.

 Use competency 3. Use the dialog above to introduce a classmate to someone else.

 D. Use competencies 4 and 5 to complete the driver's license application. Write about yourself.

DRIVER'S LICENSE APPLICATION

NAME			
Last		First	Middle

ADDRESS
Number and Street

CITY	STATE	ZIP CODE

BIRTH DATE			SEX	HEIGHT	WEIGHT
MONTH	DAY	YEAR			
			HAIR COLOR	EYE COLOR	

2 Our Community

Unit Competencies

1. Identify bank services
2. Complete deposit and withdrawal slips
3. Listen for amounts due
4. Buy money orders
5. Buy stamps and send packages

What's he doing? What's he saying? What do you think?

Read the story.

Last Thursday Duc Nguyen went to the post office. He insured a package and sent it to a friend. He also bought some stamps.

On Friday Duc went to the bank. He opened an account and deposited his money.

Starting Out

A. Practice the dialogs.

1. Last Thursday Duc went to the post office. He sent a package and bought stamps.

2. On Friday he opened a bank account and deposited some money.

➤ I want to send this to Miami.
● Do you want to insure it?
➤ Yes, please.
● That's $14.79 with insurance.
➤ I want to buy some stamps, too.
● How many do you want?
➤ Thirty, please.
● That's $9.60 for the stamps.

➤ I want to open a savings account.
● Do you want a joint account or an individual account?
➤ An individual account, please.
● OK. The minimum deposit is $250.
➤ I want to deposit $50 in cash and $200 in checks.

B. Work with a partner. Answer the questions.

1. What did Duc do at the post office?
2. What did he do at the bank?

C. Work with a partner. Use the sentences in A.
Talk about a time you went to the post office or the bank.
What did you do?

Talk It Over

 A. Kathy Noble wants to open a bank account.
Practice the dialog.

➤ Can I help you?

● Yes, I want to open a savings account. Is there a service charge?

➤ No, there's no service charge. The interest rate is 2%.

● All right, I want to open an account, please.

 B. The teller is helping Kathy complete the application form.
Practice the dialog.

➤ What's your name and your address?

● **Kathy Noble.**
1637 First Avenue.
Arlington, Virginia 20370.

➤ Your Social Security number?

● **522-70-5236.**

➤ Do you want a joint or individual account?

● **Individual.**

 C. Work with a partner.
Use the dialog in B.
Complete the application form for your partner.

$ STATE BANK   **ACCOUNT APPLICATION**

NAME _____

ADDRESS _____

CITY _____ STATE _____ ZIP CODE _____

SOCIAL SECURITY # _____ DRIVER'S LICENSE # _____

JOINT OWNER (if any) NAME _____

SOCIAL SECURITY # _____ DRIVER'S LICENSE # _____

SIGNATURE _____ JOINT OWNER SIGNATURE _____

Word Bank

A. Study the vocabulary.

Bank	Post Office	
deposit	letter	first class
withdraw	package	fourth class
account	stamp	deliver
savings	air mail	receive
individual	insured mail	send
joint		
balance		
total		
interest		
minimum		
money order		

> **Useful Language**
> Can I help you?
> (I) want to
>   (send it first class).

B. Complete the dialog. Use words from A.

✔

| air class package send yesterday |

➤ I went to the post office ___yesterday___ afternoon.

● Oh. Did you _____ a letter?

➤ No. I sent a _____ to my sister in Ohio.

● Did you send it _____ mail?

➤ No. I sent it first _____.

C. You want to send an insured package to a friend. Complete the form.

SENDER: Fill in name and address of addressee as shown on the package.
NAME
House No. and Street, Apt. No.; or Box or R.D. No. *(in care of)*, City, State, and ZIP Code
COVERAGE—Postal insurance covers (1) the value of the contents or (2) the cost of repairs. It does not cover spoilage of perishable items. Coverage may not exceed the limit fixed for the insurance fee paid.

Listening

A. Some people are at the post office.
Look and listen. Circle the kind of mail in column A.

	A		B
1.	(first class)	insured mail	__55__ ¢
2.	fourth class	insured mail	$_____
3.	fourth class	first class	$_____

Listen again. Write the amount in column B.

B. Some people are at the bank. Look and listen.
Circle the answer in column A.

	A		B
1.	(deposit)	withdrawal	$ 212.00
2.	deposit	withdrawal	$_____
3.	deposit	withdrawal	$_____

Listen again. Write the amount in column B.

C. Look and listen.
Write the information about bank savings plans.

Bank	Minimum Deposit	Service Charge	Interest Rate
City Savings	$100	none	5%
Town Bank			
National Savings		if balance is under $1,000	

D. Which bank do you want to use? Why?

Reading

A. Look and read.

Be Smart—Use the Bank!

Banks offer many services. These services can keep your money safe. That's why so many people use banks.

Bank accounts are good places to keep money. If you have a lot of cash at home, someone can take it. Your money is safer in a bank. Also, money in a bank account can earn interest. Bank accounts are also usually protected by insurance. Ask your bank if your money is insured.

Checks and money orders are good ways to pay for things. Checks are easy to write and very safe. You can carry them with you or send them in the mail safely. Never send cash in the mail. If you don't have a checking account, you can buy a money order at a bank.

You often have to pay service charges for bank services. But if you use banks, your money is usually much safer.

B. Complete the sentences.

✔

charge check insurance interest

1. Bank accounts are usually protected by ___insurance___.

2. You can send a _____ in the mail instead of cash.

3. There is usually a small service _____ for a money order.

4. Money in a bank can earn _____.

C. Work in a small group. Talk about bank services.

1. Do you use a bank? Which one? Why?
2. Which bank services do you use?

Structure Base

A. Study the examples.

I He She We You They	opened didn't open	a savings account yesterday.

B. Complete the sentences. Follow the examples in A.

1. Yesterday morning I _____mailed_____ (**mail**) a package at the post office.

2. I _____ (**not insure**) it. I _____ (**not mail**) it air mail.

3. My friend Gloria _____ (**receive**) some mail from Mexico.

4. She _____ (**open**) her mail right away.

C. Study the examples.

I	bought didn't buy	stamps last Friday.

Irregular Verbs	
buy	bought
get	got
go	went
have	had
send	sent

D. Complete the sentences.

1. Yesterday Raymond _____received_____ (**receive**) two letters from his friends in Korea.

2. But he _____ (**not receive**) any letters from his friends in Guam.

3. Later he _____ (**go**) to the post office.

4. He _____ (**buy**) air mail stamps for letters to Korea and Guam.

**E. Work with a partner. Talk about the mail.
   Follow the examples in D.**

F. Study the examples.

What	did you	do yesterday?
Where		go last week?
When		send the letter?

G. Complete the dialog. Write the correct word.

➤ Where ___did___ you _____go_____ (**go**) yesterday?

● I _____ (**go**) to the post office.

➤ What _____ you _____ (**buy**)?

● I _____ (**buy**) twenty stamps.

I _____ (**have**) several letters to send.

➤ Where _____ you _____ (**send**) the letters?

● I _____ (**send**) them to Korea.

**H. Work with a partner.
   Ask your partner what he or she did yesterday.
   Follow the sentences in G.**

I. Write your partner's answers in H.

_____

_____

Write It Down

A. Complete the deposit slip. Your account number is 91904603. Deposit three checks: one for $15.00, one for $595.75, and one for $25.75. Sign for $20.00 cash returned.

FRANKLIN NATIONAL BANK

DEPOSIT SLIP

DATE _____ 19 _____

DEPOSIT TO ACCOUNT OF _____

STREET ADDRESS _____

CITY OR TOWN   STATE   ZIP CODE

CHECKING ☐   SAVINGS ☒

_____
SIGN FOR CASH RETURNED

91904603

ACCOUNT NUMBER	DOLLARS	CENTS
CASH		
CHECKS	15	00
SUB-TOTAL	636	50
LESS CASH RETURNED		
TOTAL DEPOSIT	616	50

B. Complete the withdrawal slip. Write your savings account number. Withdraw $27.00. Sign for your withdrawal.

FRANKLIN NATIONAL BANK

WITHDRAWAL SLIP

1 FRANKLIN PLAZA
BALSAM, CA 97105

DATE _____ 19 _____

_____
NAME

_____
STREET ADDRESS

_____
ACCOUNT NUMBER

CITY OR TOWN   STATE   ZIP CODE

AMOUNT [ ]

CHECKING ☐

SAVINGS ☒   SIGNATURE _____

I. Practice the dialog.

> ➤ Excuse me. I want to open a savings account.
> ● OK. The minimum deposit is **$100.**
> ➤ What's the interest rate?
> ● It's **3%.**
> ➤ And is there a service charge?
> ● **No, there's no** service charge.

2. Use the chart. Use the dialog in I to ask Student B about a savings account. Write the information.

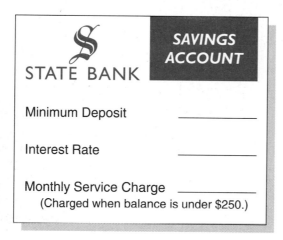

3. Student B wants information on savings accounts. Use the chart to answer the questions. Use the dialog in I.

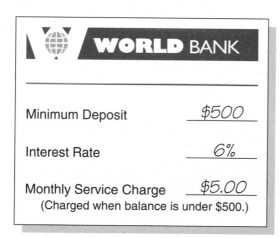

4. Switch roles. Turn to page 26. Complete 2 and 3.

I. Practice the dialog.

➤ Excuse me. I want to open a savings account.

● OK. The minimum deposit is **$100.**

➤ What's the interest rate?

● It's **3%.**

➤ And is there a service charge?

● **No, there's no** service charge.

2. Student A wants information on savings accounts. Use the chart to answer the questions. Use the dialog in I.

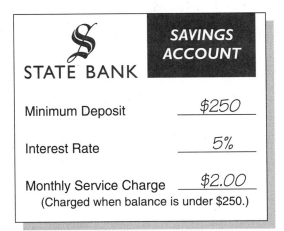

STATE BANK

SAVINGS ACCOUNT

Minimum Deposit	$250
Interest Rate	5%
Monthly Service Charge	$2.00

(Charged when balance is under $250.)

About You

3. Use the chart. Use the dialog in I to ask Student A about a savings account. Write the information.

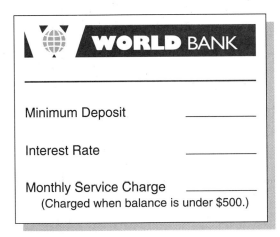

WORLD BANK

Minimum Deposit	_____
Interest Rate	_____
Monthly Service Charge	_____

(Charged when balance is under $500.)

4. Switch roles. Turn to page 25. Complete 2 and 3.

Extension

 A. Practice the dialog.

> ➤ May I help you?
> ● I need to buy a money order.
> ➤ For how much?
> ● **$10.**
> ➤ There's a 50¢ service charge.
>   Your total's **$10.50.**
> ● OK. Here's **$10.50.**
>   How do I fill it out?
> ➤ Write the name of the person to
>   receive the money at the top.
>   Then put your name and
>   address at the bottom.
> ● Thank you.
> ➤ You're welcome.

 B. Work with a partner.
Use the dialog in A to buy a money order for $100.

 C. Complete the money order.
Write City English School and the date at the top.
Write your signature and address at the bottom.

PURCHASER PLEASE COMPLETE AT ONCE.	CENTRAL SAVINGS & LOAN Gainesville, Florida	Money Order 9020 802
FILL IN THE DATE. ▶		DATE _____
WHO ARE YOU PAYING? ▶	PAY TO THE ORDER OF _____	
ENTER THE AMOUNT ▶	AMOUNT ___THE SUM 100DOLS 00CTS___	DOLLARS
SIGN, PRINT YOUR ADDRESS ▶	SIGNATURE _____	ADDRESS _____

⑆0919005331⑆241992780226⑈ 90

Can you use the competencies?

- ☐ 1. Identify bank services
- ☐ 2. Complete deposit and withdrawal slips
- ☐ 3. Listen for amounts due
- ☐ 4. Buy money orders
- ☐ 5. Buy stamps and send packages

A. Use competency I.
What can you do at the bank?
Circle the answers.

open a checking account   buy stamps

open a savings account   get interest on your savings

insure packages   keep your money safe

buy money orders   send packages air mail

mail a letter   withdraw your money

deposit some money   insure a package

B. Use competency 2. Withdraw $35.00 from your account.
Sign for your withdrawal.

FRANKLIN
NATIONAL BANK

1 FRANKLIN PLAZA
BALSAM, CA 97105

WITHDRAWAL SLIP

DATE _____ 19 _____

NAME _____

333904603

STREET ADDRESS _____
ACCOUNT NUMBER

CITY OR TOWN   STATE   ZIP CODE

AMOUNT [   ]

CHECKING ☐

SAVINGS ☒   SIGNATURE _____

C. Use competency 3.
Look and listen.
Write the amount due.

1. _32_ ¢   2. $_____   3. $_____   4. _____¢

D. Review competency 4. Complete the dialog.

✔

charge   help   money order

➤ May I ___help___ you?

● Yes, I want to buy a _____ for **$75,** please.

➤ OK. There's a $1.00 service _____.

Use competency 4.
Use the dialog above to buy a money order for $20.

E. Review competency 5. Complete the dialog.

insure   package

● I want to **send this** _____ **to Ohio.**

➤ All right. Do you want **to** _____ **it?**

● **Yes, I do.**

Use competency 5. What do you want to do at the post office? Use the dialog above to talk about it.

3 Our Country

Unit Competencies

1. Identify branches of government
2. Identify citizenship requirements
3. Complete a citizenship application
4. Describe the U.S. flag
5. Say the Pledge of Allegiance

What are the people doing? What are they saying? What do you think?

Read the story.

Ivan is becoming a U.S. citizen right now. He applied last year. First he had to fill out a long form. Second he had to submit some photographs and pay a fee. Third he had to have an interview. It was a lot of work, but he's happy he's a citizen.

Starting Out

A. Look and read.

1. This woman is a U.S. citizen.
   She's voting for legislators,
   judges, and the President.

2. These people are legislators.
   They make the laws.
   There are state legislators and
   federal legislators.

3. These people are judges.
   They hear and decide court cases.
   There are state judges and
   federal judges.

4. These people are new citizens.
   They are taking an oath of
   allegiance to the U.S.

About
You

**B. What do these people do? Use the sentences in A.
Write the letter for the answer.**

1. U.S. citizens __b__.   a. hear and decide court cases

2. Legislators _____.   ✔ b. can vote in elections

3. Judges _____.   c. make the laws

Talk It Over

To become a U.S. citizen, you must:
1. Be at least 18 years old.
2. Know how to speak, read, and write English.
3. Know U.S. history and government.
4. Live in the U.S. for at least 5 years.

A. Practice the dialog.

> ➤ I want to become a U.S. citizen.
> ● OK, **Aziza.** How old are you?
> ➤ **Eighteen.**
> ● Can you speak, read, and write English?
> ➤ **Yes, pretty well.**
> ● **Good.** Do you know U.S. history and government?
> ➤ **Yes, I studied it in school.**
> ● And how long have you lived in the United States?
> ➤ **Six years.**
> ● **Great. Then you can apply for citizenship. Go to the Immigration Office and get an application.**

B. Talk to three students. Use the dialog in A. Write the information.

Name	Age	English	U.S. History and Government	Time in the U.S.
Aziza	18	Yes	Yes	6 Years

Word Bank

A. Study the vocabulary.

Government
federal
state
judge
legislator
President

Useful Language
How long have you (lived in the U.S.)?

be able to
believe

citizen
Congress

**Branches
of Government**
judicial
legislative
executive

choose
decide
enforce

application

eligible
history
immigration
resident
vote

B. Who are these people? Write the answers on the lines.

President _____

_____

C. Talk to a partner.
What does each official in B do?

Listening

A. Listen and circle the answers.

1. Who is a citizen?   Ana   (Pablo)   Chen

2. Who wants to become a citizen?   Ana   Pablo   Chen

3. Who doesn't want to become a citizen?   Ana   Pablo   Chen

What are the people's reasons?
Listen again and match. Write the letter.

1. Pablo __b__.   a. really likes America

2. Ana _____.   ✔b. cannot return to his home country

3. Chen _____.   c. doesn't want to give up her present nationality

Listen again. Number Pablo's steps in order from 1 to 7.

_____ He turned in photographs.

_____ He became a permanent resident.

_____ He became a citizen.

___3___ He applied for citizenship.

___1___ He came to the U.S.

_____ He had an interview.

___5___ He paid a fee.

B. Work in a small group. Which students are citizens?
Which students want to become citizens? Why?

Reading

A. Look and read.

Legislative

Executive

Judicial

Three Branches of Government

The U.S. government is like a tree with three branches. The three branches are the legislative branch, the executive branch, and the judicial branch.

The legislative branch is called Congress. Congress is made up of two groups—the Senate and the House of Representatives. Both groups consider future laws. Future laws are called bills. If both groups pass a bill, it goes to the President for approval.

The President is the head of the executive branch. The President enforces laws. When Congress passes a bill, the President can sign it or veto it. When the President signs a bill, it becomes a law.

The judicial branch hears and decides cases in court. It makes sure that laws agree with the Constitution. The highest court is the Supreme Court. The President appoints judges to the Supreme Court and Congress approves each judge.

B. What does each branch do?
Write the numbers in the tree.

1. This branch makes sure laws agree with the Constitution.
2. This branch considers and passes bills.
3. This branch hears and decides cases.
4. This branch enforces the laws.

Structure Base

A. Study the examples.

I	have to	fill out an application.
We		
You		
They		
He	has to	
She		

B. What are the requirements for citizenship? Write sentences with *have to*.

> **To become a U.S. citizen, you must:**
> 1. Be at least 18 years old.
> 2. Know how to speak, read, and write English.
> 3. Know U.S. history and government.
> 4. Live in the U.S. for at least 5 years.

1. You have to be at least 18 years old.

2. _____

3. _____

4. _____

C. Work with a partner.
Talk about what you have to do to become a citizen.

D. Study the examples.

I'd	like to study U.S. history.
He'd	
She'd	
We'd	
You'd	
They'd	

E. Rogelio has a lot of plans for this year.
Follow the examples in D. Complete his list.

1. I'd like to study _____ (study) English this year.

2. I _____ (apply) for U.S. citizenship.

3. I _____ (read) more about U.S. history.

4. I _____ (learn) more about the U.S. government.

F. Work in a small group. Talk about what you'd like to do this year. Follow the sentences in E.

G. Study the examples.

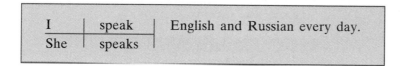

| I | speak | English and Russian every day. |
| She | speaks | |

I'm	speaking English right now.
You're	
She's	

H. Sonia wants to become a U.S. citizen.
Complete her sentences. Follow the examples in G.

1. I always _____ speak _____ (speak) English at work.

2. I _____ (learn) to read and write English now, too.

3. I _____ (study) U.S. history and government every day.

4. I usually _____ (study) with my friends.

5. Now we _____ (learn) how to apply for citizenship.

6. Right now we _____ (study) the branches of government.

Write It Down

About You

Complete this part of the U.S. citizenship application.

START HERE - Please Type or Print

Part 1.   Information about you.

Family Name	Given Name	Middle Initial

U.S. Mailing Address - Care of

Street Number and Name		Apt. Number

City	County

State	ZIP Code

Date of Birth (month/day/year)	Country of Birth

Social Security #	

Part 2.   Basis for Eligibility (check one).

a. ☐ I have been a permanent resident for at least five (5) years.

b. ☐ I have been a permanent resident for at least three (3) years and have been married to a
United States Citizen for those three years.

c. ☐ I am a permanent resident child of United States Citizen parent(s).

Part 3.   Additional information about you.

Have you been absent from the U.S. since becoming a permanent resident?   ☐ No   ☐ Yes

If you answered "Yes," complete the following. Begin with your most recent absence. If you
need more room to explain the reason for an absence or to list more trips, continue on separate paper.

Date left U.S.	Date returned	Did absence last 6 months or more?	Destination	Reason for trip
		☐ Yes ☐ No		
		☐ Yes ☐ No		
		☐ Yes ☐ No		
		☐ Yes ☐ No		

One To One

Student A

I. Practice the dialog.

➤ When did **he** become a permanent resident?
● On **July 12, 1987.**
➤ Where did **he** enter the U.S.?
● **New York.**
➤ Is **he** married?
● **Yes, he is.**
➤ Does **he** speak, read, and write English?
● **Yes, he does.**

Date you became a permanent resident (month/day/year).	Port admitted with immigrant visa or INS Office where granted adjustment of status.
7/12/87	*New York*

Citizenship
Cuban

Name on alien registration card
Ernesto Roberto Flores

Sex ☒ Male ☐ Female | Marital Status: ☐ Single ☒ Married ☐ Divorced ☐ Widowed
Can you speak, read, and write English? ☐ No ☒ Yes

About You

2. Complete the citizenship application form for Joel Martine Prevalus. Ask Student B. Follow the dialog in I.

Date you became a permanent resident (month/day/year).	Port admitted with immigrant visa or INS Office where granted adjustment of status.

Citizenship
Haitian

Name on alien registration card
Joel Martine Prevalus

Sex ☐ Male ☐ Female | Marital Status: ☐ Single ☐ Married ☐ Divorced ☐ Widowed
Can you speak, read, and write English? ☐ No ☐ Yes

3. Help Carmen Marta Torres apply for citizenship. Use the application form. Tell Student B. Follow the dialog in I.

Date you became a permanent resident (month/day/year).	Port admitted with immigrant visa or INS Office where granted adjustment of status.
5/16/90	*San Francisco*

Citizenship
Chilean

Name on alien registration card
Carmen Marta Torres

Sex ☐ Male ☒ Female | Marital Status: ☐ Single ☒ Married ☐ Divorced ☐ Widowed
Can you speak, read, and write English? ☐ No ☒ Yes

Unit 3

I. Practice the dialog.

➤ When did **he** become a permanent resident?
● On **July 12, 1987.**
➤ Where did **he** enter the U.S.?
● **New York.**
➤ Is **he** married?
● **Yes, he is.**
➤ Does **he** speak, read, and write English?
● **Yes, he does.**

Date you became a permanent resident (month/day/year). *7/12/87*	Port admitted with immigrant visa or INS Office where granted adjustment of status. *New York*
Citizenship *Cuban*	
Name on alien registration card *Ernesto Roberto Flores*	
Sex ☒ Male ☐ Female	Marital Status: ☐ Single ☒ Married ☐ Divorced ☐ Widowed
Can you speak, read, and write English? ☐ No ☒ Yes	

2. Help Joel Martine Prevalus apply for citizenship. Use the application form. Tell Student A. Follow the dialog in I.

Date you became a permanent resident (month/day/year). *3/12/92*	Port admitted with immigrant visa or INS Office where granted adjustment of status. *New York*
Citizenship *Haitian*	
Name on alien registration card *Joel Martine Prevalus*	
Sex ☒ Male ☐ Female	Marital Status: ☒ Single ☐ Married ☐ Divorced ☐ Widowed
Can you speak, read, and write English? ☐ No ☒ Yes	

3. Complete the citizenship application form for Carmen Marta Torres. Ask Student A. Follow the dialog in I.

Date you became a permanent resident (month/day/year).	Port admitted with immigrant visa or INS Office where granted adjustment of status.
Citizenship *Chilean*	
Name on alien registration card *Carmen Marta Torres*	
Sex ☐ Male ☐ Female	Marital Status: ☐ Single ☐ Married ☐ Divorced ☐ Widowed
Can you speak, read, and write English? ☐ No ☐ Yes	

Extension

A. Look and read.

The U.S flag is red, white, and blue.
The thirteen red and white stripes
are for the first thirteen states.
The fifty white stars are for the fifty U.S. states.

A pledge is a promise.
The Pledge of Allegiance is
a promise to be loyal to
the U.S. Children usually
say the Pledge of
Allegiance in school.

I pledge allegiance to the flag
of the United States of America
and to the republic
for which it stands,
one nation under God,
indivisible, with liberty
and justice for all.

B. Answer the questions.

1. What color is the U.S. flag?
2. How many stripes are there?
3. What color are the stripes?
4. How many stars are there?
5. What color are the stars?

**C. Work with a partner.
Take turns saying the Pledge of Allegiance.**

Can you use the competencies?

☐ 1. Identify branches of government
☐ 2. Identify citizenship requirements
☐ 3. Complete a citizenship application
☐ 4. Describe the U.S. flag
☐ 5. Say the Pledge of Allegiance

A. Use competency I.
Complete the sentences.
Write the letter for the answer.

1. The legislative branch __c__.
2. The judicial branch _____.
3. The executive branch _____.

a. includes the President
b. hears and decides court cases
✔ c. makes laws

B. Use competency 2.
Complete the sentences.
✔

| history   English   5   18 |

To become a U.S. citizen, you must:

1. Be at least __18__ years old.
2. Know how to speak, read, and write _____ .
3. Know U.S. _____ and government.
4. Live in the U.S. for at least _____ years.

C. Use competency 3. Complete the citizenship application. Write about yourself.

Date you became a permanent resident (month/day/year).	Port admitted with immigrant visa or INS Office where granted adjustment of status.
Citizenship	
Name on alien registration card	

Sex ☐ Male ☐ Female	Marital Status: ☐ Single ☐ Married ☐ Divorced ☐ Widowed
Can you speak, read, and write English? ☐ No ☐ Yes	

D. Use competency 4. Write about the U.S. flag.

✔

fifty   red   thirteen   white

1. The U.S. flag has _____thirteen_____ stripes.

2. The stripes are _____ and white.

3. The flag has _____ stars.

4. The stars are _____ .

E. Review competency 5. Complete the Pledge of Allegiance.

✔

flag   liberty   nation   republic

I pledge allegiance to the _____flag_____

of the United States of America,

and to the _____ for which it stands,

one _____ under God, indivisible,

with _____ and justice for all.

Use competency 5. Say the Pledge of Allegiance.

4 Daily Living

Unit Competencies

1. Describe your native country

2. Talk about why you came to the U.S.

3. Describe how you felt when you came to the U.S.

4. Talk about where you have lived

What are the people doing? What are they saying? What do you think?

Practice the dialog.

➤ Where did you grow up?

● I grew up in Mexico, on a farm in the country.

➤ Really? What was it like?

● It was a quiet place with a river nearby.

➤ Did you swim in the river?

● Sure. We swam and fished. We hiked in the mountains, too. It was a wonderful place to grow up.

➤ Why did you leave?

● We left because the farm didn't do well. I felt terrible.

➤ Oh. That's too bad.

Starting Out

A. People are talking about their native countries. Where did they grow up? Practice the dialogs.

➤ I grew up in a village near the ocean.

● I bet it was beautiful there.

➤ It was. There was no high school. I had to move.

➤ I grew up in a small town in the mountains.

● Oh. Did you like living there?

➤ Yes, but there was fighting in my country. We had to leave.

➤ I grew up in a big, crowded city.

● Wow! Was it exciting?

➤ Yes, but it was noisy and dangerous, too.

➤ I grew up on a farm in the country.

● Was it peaceful?

➤ Yes, but there was no rain. We had to move to the city.

About You

B. Work with a partner. Answer the questions.

1. Where did the people grow up? Why did the people leave?
2. Where did you grow up? What did you like about it? Why did you leave?

Talk It Over

A. Practice the dialog.

> ➤ **Alex,** where do you live?
> ● **Chicago.**
> ➤ Really? Did you grow up there?
> ● No. I grew up in **a town in Mexico.**
> ➤ Why did you come here?
> ● I wanted **to study in the U.S.**
> ➤ How did you get here?
> ● By **bus.**

B. Talk to three students. Use the dialog in A. Write the answers.

Name	Where did you grow up?	Why did you come here?	How did you get here?	Where do you live now?
Alex	Mexico	to study	by bus	Chicago

Word Bank

A. Study the vocabulary.

		Feelings	lake
beautiful	peaceful		
boring	quiet	comfortable	mountains
busy	small	excited	ocean
clean		happy	river
crowded	boat	lonely	
dangerous	bus	lucky	city
dirty	car	scared	farm
exciting	plane		village
large	train	coast	town
noisy	truck	country	

B. Work in a small group. Is the picture the same or different from where you have lived? How is it the same? How is it different? Use words from A.

C. Work with a group. Discuss the questions.

1. Where do you live? What do you like about it?
2. Do you always want to live here? Where else would you like to live?

Listening

 A. Where did the people grow up?
Look, listen, and number the pictures.

_____ |1|_____   _____

 B. Look and listen. Dora, Truc, and Benito are talking.
They're telling the class about their native countries.
Circle the places where they are from.

1. Dora	(Ecuador)	Bolivia
2. Truc	Hong Kong	Vietnam
3. Benito	Mexico	Guatemala

Listen again. Circle how they felt when they arrived in
the U.S.

1. Dora	lucky	(scared)
2. Truc	hopeful	sad
3. Benito	comfortable	lonely

Listen again. What are they doing now?
Complete the sentences. Write the letter.

1. Dora __c__.   a. works in a hospital

2. Truc ____.   b. has a shop

3. Benito ____.   ✔c. goes to school

Reading

A. Read the story.

My name is Anton. I was born in Russia in 1960. I grew up in the far eastern part of Russia. I lived in a small fishing village on the coast. It was very peaceful, but it was cold in the winter. In 1980 I moved to town to go to school.

In 1990 I moved to Anchorage, Alaska. A year later I got a job with a fishing company. Anchorage is much larger than my village in Siberia. At first I felt lonely, but now I'm happy to live in the United States. And I like speaking English at work.

B. Complete the time line. Write the letter in the circle.

a. He got a job with a fishing company.
b. He moved to town to go to school.
✔ c. He was born in Russia.
d. He moved to Anchorage, Alaska.

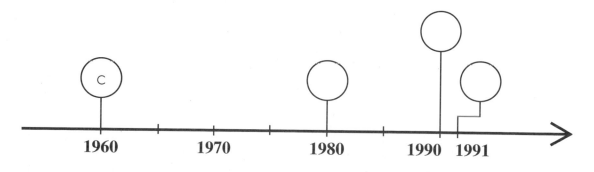

Structure Base

A. Study the examples.

Where	did you	grow up?
When		come to the U.S.?
How		feel?

Irregular Verbs	
come	came
feel	felt
grow up	grew up
see	saw
swim	swam

I	grew up in Mexico.
	came to the U.S. in 1987.
	felt excited.

B. Complete the dialog. Read the answers. Use words from A to write the questions.

➤ <u>Where did you grow up?</u>

● I grew up in **Hong Kong.**

➤ _____

● I came to the U.S. in **1990.**

➤ _____

● I felt **excited.**

➤ Are you happy here?

● Yes, I am. But sometimes I miss Hong Kong.

C. Work with a partner. Use the dialog in B to talk about yourself.

D. Study the examples.

> Did you swim in the lake?

Yes,	I	did.
No,		didn't.

E. Complete the dialog. Write *did* or *didn't*.

➤ Did Pedro live in Mexico City?

● Yes, he _____did_____.

➤ Did he like it?

● Yes, he _____.

➤ Did he write to you then?

● No, he _____.

➤ Did you write to him?

● No, I _____.

F. Complete the dialog. Follow the examples in D.

➤ __Did_____ Pedro _____visit_____ (visit) the U.S. last year?
● Yes, he did. He visited our family.

➤ _____ he _____ (come) by plane?
● No. He came by train.

➤ _____ he _____ (stay) with you?
● No, he didn't. He stayed with our aunt.

➤ _____ you _____ (see) him?
● Yes. I saw him at our aunt's house.

Write It Down

A. Look at the time line. Read the story.

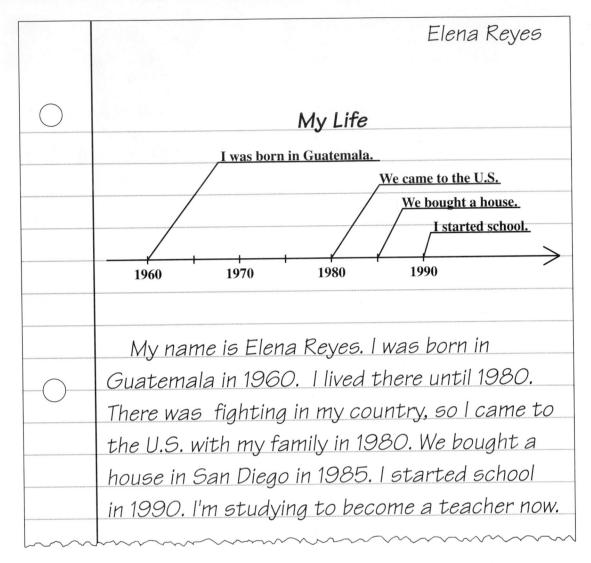

Elena Reyes

My Life

- I was born in Guatemala.
- We came to the U.S.
- We bought a house.
- I started school.

1960   1970   1980   1990

My name is Elena Reyes. I was born in Guatemala in 1960. I lived there until 1980. There was fighting in my country, so I came to the U.S. with my family in 1980. We bought a house in San Diego in 1985. I started school in 1990. I'm studying to become a teacher now.

B. Make a time line about yourself.

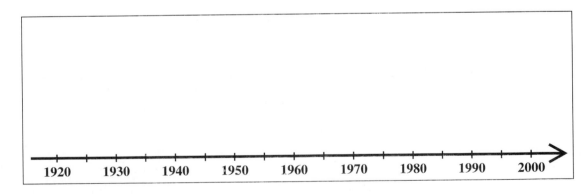

1920   1930   1940   1950   1960   1970   1980   1990   2000

**C. Look at your time line.
Write your story on a sheet of paper.**

1. Practice the dialog.

➤ Where's **Li-ming** from?
● **He's** from **China.**
➤ Why did **he** leave **China?**
● He wanted to go to school here.

2. Where are they from? Why did they leave?
Ask Student B. Follow the dialog in 1. Write the information.

Li-ming   Van   Marita

China _____   _____   _____

He wanted to go   _____   _____

to school here.   _____   _____

3. Where are they from? Why did they leave?
Tell Student B. Follow the dialog in 1.

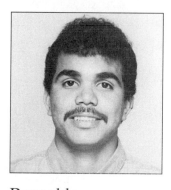  

Reynaldo   Soo Ha   Jean

Nicaragua   Korea   Haiti

He wanted a job in   She wanted to   He wanted to find
his family's business.   study English.   a job.

One To One

1. Practice the dialog.

➤ Where's **Li-ming** from?

● **He's** from **China.**

➤ Why did **he** leave **China?**

● He wanted to go to school here.

2. Where are they from? Why did they leave?
Tell Student A. Follow the dialog in 1.

Li-ming

China

He wanted to go
to school here.

Van

Cambodia

There was fighting
in his country.

Marita

Mexico

She wanted to join
her family.

3. Where are they from? Why did they leave?
Ask Student A. Follow the dialog in 1. Write the information.

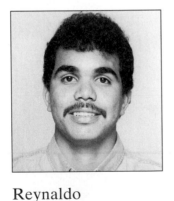

Reynaldo

Nicaragua

He wanted a job in

his family's business.

Soo Ha

_____

_____

_____

Jean

_____

_____

_____

Extension

A. Look at the map.
Where did you live?
Where do you live now?

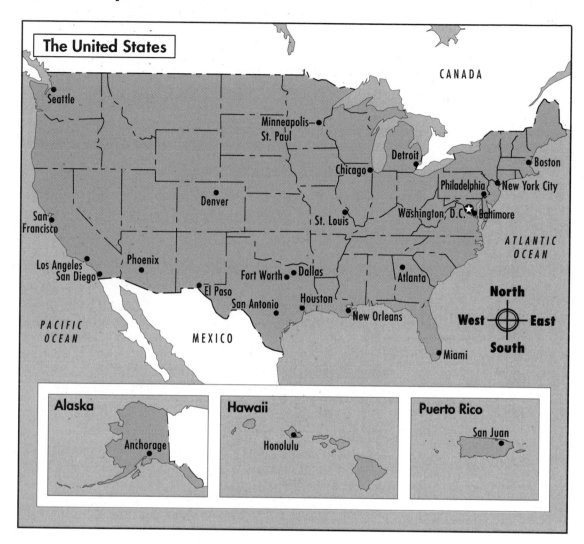

B. Josh and Ricardo live in New York.
Josh is asking Ricardo about other places he lived.
Practice the dialog.

➤ Where did you live when you came to the U.S.?
● I lived in **Miami** for **a short time.**
➤ Then where did you live?
● I lived in **Boston** for **two years.**
➤ When did you move to **New York?**
● In **1989.**

C. Work with a partner.
Use the dialog in B to talk about yourselves.

Can you use the competencies?

☐ 1. Describe your native country
☐ 2. Talk about why you came to the U.S.
☐ 3. Describe how you felt when you came to the U.S.
☐ 4. Talk about where you have lived

A. Review competency I.
Complete the story.

✔

| beautiful   grew up   ocean   village |

My name is **Hector Delgado.** I'm from **Puerto Rico.** I ____grew up____

in a _____ **near the ocean.** It was a _____

place. I swam in the _____ **and fished.**

Check Up

Use competency I.
Use the story above to talk about your native country.

B. Review competencies 2 and 3. Complete the dialog.

✔

feel   job   lonely   why

➤ **Hector,** _____why_____ did you leave **Puerto Rico?**

● **My family was very poor. My father wanted to find a better**

_____ **in the U.S.**

➤ How did you _____ when you came here?

● I felt **excited. But I was scared and** _____, **too.**

Use competencies 2 and 3.
Use the dialog above to talk about yourself.

C. Review competency 4. Complete the dialog.

✔

live   like   move

➤ **Hector,** where did you _____live_____ when you came to the U.S.?

● **Miami. But I didn't like it.** I lived there for **two years. Then I moved.**

➤ Where did you _____ to?

● I moved to **Chicago.**

➤ Did you _____ it?

● **Yes, I did.**

Use competency 4.
Use the dialog above to talk about yourself.

Unit Competencies

1. Read recipes and package directions
2. Listen to supermarket ads
3. Read supermarket ads
4. Identify sales and coupons

What are the people doing? What are they saying? What do you think?

Practice the dialog.

➤ What are we having for dinner?

● Let's have spaghetti.

➤ That sounds good. Do we have everything we need?

● No. I have to go to the store.

➤ Let's make a shopping list. What do we need?

● Let's see. Two cans of tomato sauce, some mushrooms, two onions, and a pound of ground beef for the sauce. And we need a box of spaghetti.

➤ Do we have any cheese?

● No, we don't. I have to get some cheese, too.

Starting Out

A. Look and read.

➤ Let's try the new stew recipe for dinner tonight, Marta.

● All right, Pablo. But first I have to go to the store.

● Do I have everything? Carrots, celery, beef, peppers, onions, and noodles. Good. Here's a coupon for the noodles.

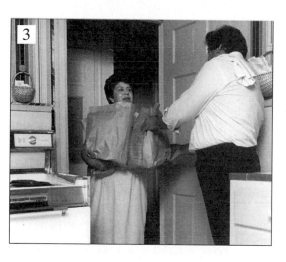

● Hi, I'm back. Could you help me with the groceries?

➤ Sure, give them to me.

● Put them away. Then we can start to cook.

➤ The recipe says: First cook the meat in a pot. Then cut up the vegetables and put them in the pot. Add water. Cook for two hours. Serve over noodles.

B. Work with a partner. Answer the questions.

1. What are they having for dinner? What did she buy?
2. What do you like to cook? How do you cook it?
3. Where do you buy your groceries? Do you make a shopping list? Do you use coupons? Why or why not?

Talk It Over

Chicken

Chicken with Garlic Tomato Sauce

1 chicken, cut in pieces
2 tablespoons of oil
½ onion, chopped
½ green pepper, chopped

1 chopped clove of garlic
1 large can of tomatoes
½ cup of chicken broth
½ teaspoon of oregano

First heat the oil in a pan. Cook the chicken in the oil. Put the chicken in a dish.

Next cook the onion, green pepper, and garlic in the pan. Put them in the dish with the chicken. Put the tomatoes, chicken broth, and oregano in the dish, too.

Cover the dish. Bake at 350° for 1 hour.

Serves 2-4 people.

A. Practice the dialog.

➤ What do you want for dinner, **Kim?**
● How about **chicken with garlic tomato sauce?**
➤ That sounds good! What do **we** need to buy?
● Well, **we** need **some chicken, a can of chicken broth, and some oil.**
➤ What else do **we** need? Do **we** need any **vegetables?**
● **Yes, we do. We need an onion, a green pepper, and a large can of tomatoes.**
➤ Do **we** need **garlic and oregano?**
● **No, we don't. We have those.**

B. Talk to three students. Use the dialog in A to talk about what you want for dinner. Write the answers.

Name	Food	Shopping List
Kim	chicken with garlic tomato sauce	chicken, chicken broth, oil, onion, green pepper, a can of tomatoes

Word Bank

A. Study the vocabulary.

coupon	**Directions**	**Cooking Utensils**
recipe	add	bowl
	bake	pan
Main Dishes	cook	pot
omelet	cover	spatula
pizza	cut (up)	
soup	mix	
spaghetti	stir	
stew		

Ingredients
celery
garlic
mushrooms
noodles
peppers
potatoes
tomato sauce

Useful Language
First . . .
Next . . .
Then . . .
After that . . .
Last . . .
Finally . . .

B. Look at the pictures. What are they? Use words from A to write the names.

1. ___spatula___   2. _____   3. _____   4. _____

C. Work with a partner. Look at the main dishes in A. Which main dishes do you make? How do you make them?

Listening

A. Listen to the cooking show. It's about making an omelet. Circle the ingredients.

(eggs)   celery   milk   water

garlic   cheese   peppers   potatoes

Listen again. Number the directions from 1 to 5.

__1__   Put two eggs in a bowl and stir them.

_____   Cover the pan for three or four minutes.

_____   Add milk and water, and put the eggs into a pan.

_____   Cook the eggs on low heat for five minutes.

_____   Put the cheese on top of the eggs.

B. Look and listen. Write what's on sale in column A.

✔

| butter | chicken | milk | oranges | cheese | potatoes |

	A	B
Food Fair	__cheese__ _____ _____	$ __2.19__ a package ____¢ a half-gallon ____¢ a pound
FRESH Way	_____ _____ _____	____¢ a pound ____¢ a pound ____¢ a pound

Listen again. Write the prices in column B.

Reading

A. Many foods have cooking directions on the package. Look and read.

To mix the dough:
Put the dough mix in a bowl.
Add 1 cup of warm water and mix it.
Cover it for 5 minutes.

To prepare the crust:
Spread the dough on the pizza pan.

To add the sauce and toppings:
Put the pizza sauce on the dough.
Put the cheese on the top.
Cut up some onions, peppers, mushrooms, or other vegetables and add them to the pizza.
Bake for 20 minutes.

B. Use the pizza package. Number the directions from 1 to 8.

_____ Put the sauce on the dough.

_____ Bake for twenty minutes.

_____ Cover it for five minutes.

___1___ Put the dough mix in a bowl.

_____ Spread the dough on the pan.

_____ Cut up and add some vegetables.

_____ Put the cheese on top.

_____ Add water and mix.

C. Answer the questions.

1. Do the directions sound easy? Why do you think so?
2. Do you make foods with directions on the package? What foods?

Structure Base

A. Study the examples.

| Do you want any | onions?
celery? |
|---|---|

| Yes, I want some | onions.
celery. |
|---|---|

| No, I don't want any | onions.
celery. |
|---|---|

B. Complete the dialog.
Use words from A to write the questions.

➤ Let's make some vegetable soup for dinner.

● That sounds good. <u>Do you want any</u> potatoes in it?

➤ Sure. I love potatoes. _____ celery?

● No, I don't like celery. _____ onions?

➤ No, that's OK. _____ carrots?

● Yes. I think carrots would be good.

C. Complete the dialog. Write *some* or *any*.

➤ What else do you want in the soup?

● Well, I'd like _____<u>some</u>_____ onions. And I'd like _____

tomatoes, too. But I don't want _____ meat.

➤ I don't want _____ meat, either. But I'd like

_____ garlic. How about you?

● No. I don't want _____ garlic. I hate it!

D. Study the examples.

Wash	the vegetables.
Cut up	
Cook	

E. Look at the package of rice. Follow the examples in D.

✔

add   cover   put   boil   cook

Rightway RICE

Directions:

1. _Boil_____ 2 cups of water in a large pot.

2. _____ 1 cup of rice into the pot.

3. _____ salt.

4. _____ the pot.

5. _____ it on low heat for 25 minutes.

Write It Down

A. Read the grocery store ad.

B. What groceries do you want to buy at Food Fair? Write your shopping list.

1. **You want to know the prices at Save-A-Lot. Your partner has the Save-A-Lot ad. Practice the dialog.**

   ➤ How much **is milk** at **Save-A-Lot?**
   ● **It's 95¢ a half-gallon.**

2. **How much is the food at Save-A-Lot? Ask Student B. Follow the dialog in I. Write the prices.**

Shopping List

milk	95¢	a half-gallon
orange juice	¢	a can
bread	¢	a loaf
eggs	¢	a dozen

3. **How much is the food at Food Mart? Tell Student B. Follow the dialog in I.**

Food Mart

LOW PRICES

Loaf of Bread
79¢
Bread

Frozen Orange Juice
12-ounce can
75¢

Orange JUICE

MILK
89¢
Milk
half-gallon

Eggs
Dozen Eggs
70¢

1. **Your partner wants to know the prices at Save-A-Lot. You have the Save-A-Lot ad. Practice the dialog.**

   ➤ How much **is milk** at **Save-A-Lot?**
   ● It's 95¢ a half-gallon.

2. **How much is the food at Save-A-Lot? Tell Student A. Follow the dialog in I.**

SAVE-A-LOT

LOW PRICES

Milk half-gallon **95¢**

Dozen Eggs **85¢**

Loaf of Bread **99¢**

Orange JUICE
Frozen Orange Juice 12-ounce can **69¢**

3. **How much is the food at Food Mart? Ask Student A. Follow the dialog in I. Write the prices.**

SHOPPING LIST

milk	89¢ a half-gallon
orange juice	___¢ a can
bread	___¢ a loaf
eggs	___¢ a dozen

Extension

A. Look and read.

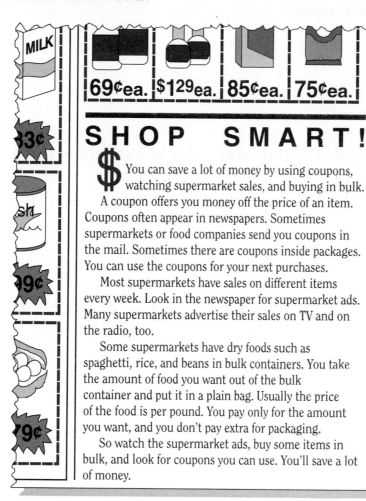

69¢ea. | $1²⁹ea. | 85¢ea. | 75¢ea.

SHOP SMART!

$ You can save a lot of money by using coupons, watching supermarket sales, and buying in bulk. A coupon offers you money off the price of an item. Coupons often appear in newspapers. Sometimes supermarkets or food companies send you coupons in the mail. Sometimes there are coupons inside packages. You can use the coupons for your next purchases.

Most supermarkets have sales on different items every week. Look in the newspaper for supermarket ads. Many supermarkets advertise their sales on TV and on the radio, too.

Some supermarkets have dry foods such as spaghetti, rice, and beans in bulk containers. You take the amount of food you want out of the bulk container and put it in a plain bag. Usually the price of the food is per pound. You pay only for the amount you want, and you don't pay extra for packaging.

So watch the supermarket ads, buy some items in bulk, and look for coupons you can use. You'll save a lot of money.

New Day
Dishwashing Liquid

Save 30¢
on 16 oz. or larger bottle

| MANUFACTURER'S COUPON |
| NO EXPIRATION |

B. Read the sentences. Write *yes* or *no*.

yes   1. Coupons appear in newspapers.

_____   2. Supermarkets never have sales.

_____   3. Bulk foods cost less than packaged foods.

_____   4. The coupon is for New Day Dishwashing Liquid.

_____   5. The dishwashing liquid costs more with the coupon.

C. Work with a small group. Answer the questions.

[About You]

1. Where do you see coupons? Do you use them?
2. Where do you buy groceries? Do you buy items on sale?
3. Do you buy any items in bulk? What items do you buy?

Can you use the competencies?

☐ 1. Read recipes and package directions
☐ 2. Listen to supermarket ads
☐ 3. Read supermarket ads
☐ 4. Identify sales and coupons

A. Review competency I. Complete the recipe directions.

✔

| add   bake   pan   put   mix |

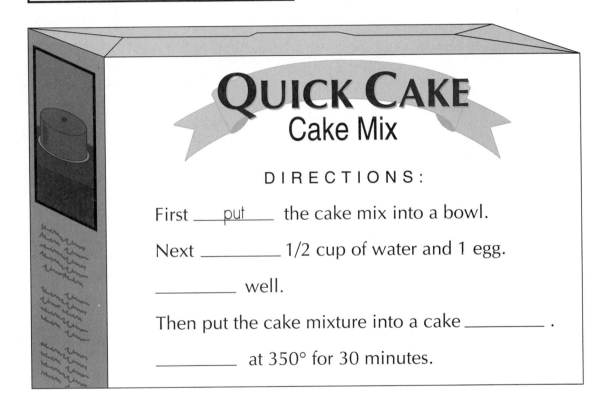

QUICK CAKE
Cake Mix

D I R E C T I O N S :

First ___put___ the cake mix into a bowl.

Next _____ 1/2 cup of water and 1 egg.

_____ well.

Then put the cake mixture into a cake _____ .

_____ at 350° for 30 minutes.

Check Up

Use competency I. Use the recipe above.
Number the directions from I to 5.

_____ Add water and an egg.

___I___ Put the cake mix into a bowl.

_____ Bake at 350° for 30 minutes.

_____ Put the cake mixture into a pan.

_____ Mix well.

B. Use competency 2. Look and listen.
   What's on sale? Write the prices.

Supermarket	Food	Price
1. Big's Market	mushrooms	_99_ ¢ a pound
2. William's Grocery	onions	_____ ¢ a pound
3. Super Save Foods	tomato sauce	_____ ¢ a can

C. Review competencies 3 and 4.
   Read the ad and the coupon.

Use competencies 3 and 4. Use the ad and coupon above.
Read the questions. Circle the answers.

1. What's the name of the supermarket having the sale?

   Delicious Foods   (Jesse Foods)   Spicy Brand

2. How much are the cookies?

   $1.49 a box   49¢ a box $2.19 a pound

3. What kind of cheese is on sale?

   Jesse Foods   Spicy   American

4. What's the coupon for?

   dishwashing liquid   tomato sauce   cookies

5. How much money off do you get with the coupon?

   30¢   49¢   10¢

6 Shopping

Unit Competencies

1. Comparison shop
2. Identify forms of payment
3. Ask for refunds and exchanges
4. Identify sales tax
5. Read clothing care labels

What are the people doing? What are they saying? What do you think?

Practice the dialog.

➤ This looks like a good tape player.
● How much is it?
➤ $49.95.
● This one is cheaper. It's only $39.95.
➤ But the more expensive one has a radio.
● You're right. That's nice.
➤ Let's think about it. We can come back tomorrow.

Starting Out

A. Practice the dialogs.

➤ Excuse me. I want a vacuum cleaner.

● Well, we have several models. Here's one for $79.95. There's a bigger model for $99.95.

➤ I'll take the cheaper one. Do you have layaway?

● Yes. We also accept cash, checks, and credit cards.

➤ I'll put it on layaway.

➤ Can I help you?

● Yes. I need some motor oil. How much is this oil?

➤ It's $12.90 per case.

● Hmmm. That's more expensive than I thought.

➤ Well, this motor oil goes on sale next week.

● Thanks. I'll come back next week and get it then.

B. Answer the questions.

1. What is the man buying? How is he paying for it?
2. How much is the motor oil? Is the woman buying it today? Why not?

C. Work with a partner. Talk about the last time you went shopping. Did you buy anything? What was it?

Talk It Over

 A. Practice the dialog.

> ➤ I'd like to return **this sweater.**
> ● Do you have the receipt?
> ➤ **Yes, I do.**
> ● What's the reason for the return?
> ➤ **It's too large.**
> ● OK. Would you like a refund or an exchange?
> ➤ **A refund,** please.
> ● All right. Please complete this form and sign it.
> ➤ Thank you.

 **B. Work with a partner. Use the dialog in A.
Return these items.**

Item	Reason	Refund or Exchange
shirt	It's the wrong size.	exchange
lamp	It doesn't work.	refund
shoes	They're too small.	exchange

**C. Work with a partner.
What do you need to return?
Use the dialog in A to return it.**

Word Bank

A. Study the vocabulary.

Clothing Care
dry clean
gentle cycle
hand wash
machine wash
washing machine

drip dry
dryer
dry flat
iron
line dry
tumble dry

Useful Language
Well, . . .
I'll take it.
It's too (large).
It's the wrong (size).

Shopping
credit card
exchange
expensive
layaway

refund
return
sales tax
subtotal
taxable

B. Work in a small group. Read the price tags and care labels. Which shirt do you want to buy? Why?

$29.95

Machine wash
Tumble dry

$19.99

Hand wash
Drip dry

Listening

A. Dean and Sue are shopping for a sweater for their mother. Look, listen, and write the price in column A.

	A	**B**
1.	$19.99	_____
2.	_____	_____

Listen again. How should you wash the sweater? Write *machine wash* or *hand wash* in column B.

Listen again. Why did they buy the white sweater? Circle the reasons.

Their mother can machine wash it.

It's larger than the other one.

It's too expensive.

It's their mother's favorite color.

B. Look, listen, and complete the return forms.

1.

Z-MART RETURN

Item Returned: ___towels___

Reason for Return: _wrong color_

Refund   Exchange

Receipt: Yes   No

2.

Z-MART RETURN

Item Returned: _____

Reason for Return: _____

Refund   Exchange

Receipt: Yes   No

Reading

A. Look and read.

$Smart $Shopper

Sales Tax Works for You

We pay sales tax on many different items. Clothing and gasoline are taxable. Most household products and supplies are taxable. New and used cars, appliances, and furniture are all taxable, too.

Most sales tax goes to city, state, and county governments. It pays for different public services. Sales tax is used to build hospitals, roads, parks, and playgrounds.

The money may support public schools and health programs. It may help pay for public transportation.

Tax rates in different states vary. And different states tax different things. For example, in Texas, food is not taxed. In Illinois, food is taxed, but at a lower rate than other items.

A few states don't have sales tax. Does your state have sales tax? How much is it?

Find out so you can be a "Smart Shopper."

B. Read the sentences. Write *yes* or *no*.

_____no_____ 1. Most sales tax goes to the federal government.

_____ 2. Gasoline is not taxable.

_____ 3. Taxes pay for public schools.

_____ 4. The sales tax is the same in all states in the U.S.

C. Look at the receipt. Answer the questions.

1. Which items are taxable? Circle them on the receipt.
2. How much is the tax? Circle it on the receipt.
3. How much is sales tax where you live?
4. Is food taxed where you live? If it is, is all food taxed or only some food?

Greenway Grocery

yogurt	$.53
(toothpaste)	$1.69 txbl
soup	$.47
milk	$1.19
paper towels	$3.00 txbl
popcorn	$1.69
lightbulb	$.79 txbl
Subtotal	$9.36
Tax	$.32
Total	$9.68

Structure Base

A. Study the examples.

The red shirt is	bigger than cheaper than heavier than nicer than better than worse than	the blue shirt.

B. Look at the pictures. Complete the sentences. Follow the pattern in A.

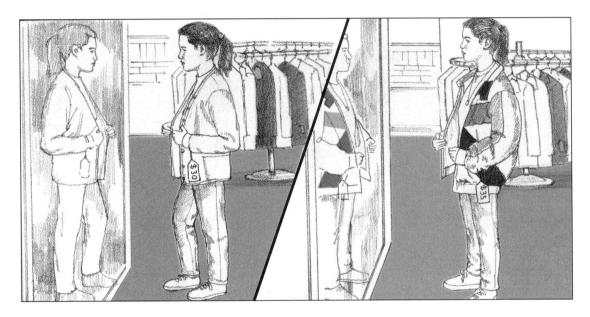

1. The **sweater** is _____*cheaper than*_____ **(cheap)** the **jacket.**

2. The **jacket** is _____ **(big)** the **sweater.**

3. The **sweater** is _____ **(small)** the **jacket.**

4. The **sweater** is _____ **(soft)** the **jacket.**

5. The **sweater** is _____ **(good)** the **jacket.**

C. Study the examples.

The red shirt is	more comfortable than more expensive than	the blue shirt.

D. Look at the pictures in B. Complete the sentences.
Follow the examples in C.

1. The **sweater** is <u>more comfortable than</u> **(comfortable)**
   the **jacket.**

2. The **jacket** is _____ **(expensive)**
   the **sweater.**

3. The **jacket** is _____ **(colorful)**
   the **sweater.**

4. The **jacket** is _____ **(attractive)**
   the **sweater.**

E. Look at the shirts. Compare them.
Write three sentences. Follow the sentences in B and D.

$8.99 $6.99

_____

_____

_____

F. Work with a partner. Talk about clothes you like.
Why do you like them? Follow the sentences in B and D.

Write It Down

A. Magali and Frank need to clean these clothes. Read the clothing care labels.

1.

Hand Wash
Cold Water Only
Drip Dry

2.

Machine Wash
Warm Water
Tumble Dry

3.

Machine Wash
Cool Water
Line Dry

4.

Dry Clean Only
Warm Iron

5.

Machine Wash
Cold Water
Dry Gentle Cycle

6.

Hand Wash Only
Cold Water
Dry Flat

About You

B. This is how Magali and Frank want to clean the clothes. Tell them if it's right or wrong. Write _right_ or _wrong_.

1. They want to wash the sweater
   in the washing machine.   _____wrong_____

2. They want to dry the skirt in the dryer.   _____

3. They want to dry clean the tie.   _____

4. They want to wash the dress in cool water.   _____

5. They want to dry the shirt on gentle cycle.   _____

6. They want to wash the blouse
   in the washing machine.   _____

7. They want to wash the sweater in hot water.   _____

8. They want to dry the sweater flat.   _____

9. They're going to use a hot iron on the tie.   _____

I. Practice the dialog.

➤ I'd like to return **this shirt.** I have the receipt.

● Why do you need to return **it?**

➤ **It's the wrong size.**

● Would you like to exchange **it**
  or would you like a refund?

➤ **I'd like to exchange it.**

2. You are a clerk at Z-Mart.
Student B wants to return three things.
Follow the dialog in I. Complete the forms.

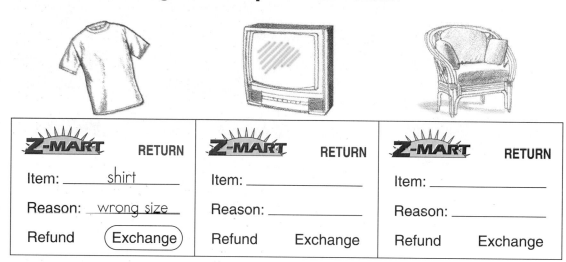

Z-MART RETURN	**Z-MART** RETURN	**Z-MART** RETURN
Item: _____shirt_____	Item: _____	Item: _____
Reason: _wrong size_	Reason: _____	Reason: _____
Refund (Exchange)	Refund Exchange	Refund Exchange

 About You

3. You want to return three things to Z-Mart.
Student B is the store clerk. Follow the dialog in I.

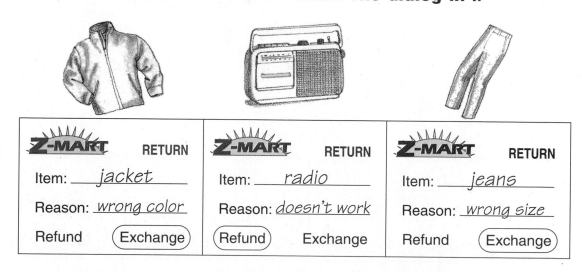

Z-MART RETURN	**Z-MART** RETURN	**Z-MART** RETURN
Item: ___jacket___	Item: ___radio___	Item: ___jeans___
Reason: _wrong color_	Reason: _doesn't work_	Reason: _wrong size_
Refund (Exchange)	(Refund) Exchange	Refund (Exchange)

4. Switch roles. Turn to page 82. Complete 2 and 3.

I. Practice the dialog.

➤ I'd like to return **this shirt.** I have the receipt.

● Why do you need to return **it?**

➤ **It's the wrong size.**

● Would you like to exchange **it**
or would you like a refund?

➤ **I'd like to exchange it.**

2. You want to return three things to Z-Mart. Student A is the store clerk. Follow the dialog in I.

Z-MART RETURN	**Z-MART** RETURN	**Z-MART** RETURN
Item: _shirt_	Item: _TV_	Item: _chair_
Reason: _wrong size_	Reason: _doesn't work_	Reason: _wrong color_
Refund (Exchange)	(Refund) Exchange	Refund (Exchange)

3. You are a clerk at Z-Mart. Student A wants to return three things. Follow the dialog in I. Complete the forms.

Z-MART RETURN	**Z-MART** RETURN	**Z-MART** RETURN
Item: _____	Item: _____	Item: _____
Reason: _____	Reason: _____	Reason: _____
Refund Exchange	Refund Exchange	Refund Exchange

4. Switch roles. Turn to page 8I. Complete 2 and 3.

Extension

A. Read the article.

Different Ways to Pay

In most stores there are several ways to pay for things. You can use cash, a check, a credit card, or layaway. Each way has good and bad points.

When you pay with cash or check, you pay the total price. There are never any extra fees. If you don't have enough cash with you, you can write a check. But what can you do when you don't have enough money in cash or in your checking account?

One thing you can do is use a credit card. The credit card company pays the store for the item. Then you pay the credit card company back. You have to pay the credit card company the full amount by a certain date. If you don't, you pay interest. Interest on credit cards is very high. However, with credit, you can pay for something a little at a time.

Another way to pay a little at a time is to buy on layaway. You only pay part of the total price at first, but the store keeps your item. They "lay it away" (keep it for you) until you pay the rest of the bill. Over time, you pay the rest. Then you can take your item from the store. Not every store offers layaway.

Which form of payment is better for you? When you buy something, think about the cost, your budget, and your other monthly needs when you decide how to pay.

B. Answer the questions.

1. How many ways can shoppers pay for things?
2. If you don't have enough money in your checking account or in cash, how can you pay?
3. When would you pay cash? When would you pay with a check? When would you use layaway?

C. Work with a small group. Talk about these items. How would you pay for them? Why?

$399.00 $69.99 $15.99

Can you use the competencies?

- ☐ 1. Comparison shop
- ☐ 2. Identify forms of payment
- ☐ 3 Ask for refunds and exchanges
- ☐ 4. Identify sales tax
- ☐ 5. Read clothing care labels

A. Review competencies I and 2. Complete the dialog.

✔

| buy   expensive   sale |

➤ Look! There's a little tape player on ___sale___ for $29.

● Hmmm. That other tape player has a radio.

   But it's more _____. It's $39.

➤ Well, **I don't want a radio** I'm going to _____ the **cheaper** one.

   I'll put it on layaway.

Check Up

**Use competencies I and 2. Use the dialog above.
Shop for a tape player. Which one do you want?
How will you pay?**

B. Review competency 3. Complete the dialog.

✔

| exchange   reason   return   wrong |

➤ I want to _____return_____ **this shirt.** Here's the receipt.

● What's the _____ for the return?

➤ **It's the** _____ **size.**

● Do you want an _____ or a refund?

➤ **A refund,** please.

Use competency 3. Use the dialog above to return something

C. Use competency 4. Look at the receipt. Answer the questions. Circle the answers.

1. Which item is taxable?

   bread   eggs   dishwashing liquid

2. How much is the tax?

   $2.19   11¢   82¢

```
~~~~~~~~~~~~~~~~~~~~~~~~~~
          ❖
        FRESH
         Way
bread          $1.69
doz. eggs      $1.19
dishwashing
   liquid      $2.19 txbl

SUBTOTAL       $5.07
TAX            $ .11
TOTAL          $5.18
~~~~~~~~~~~~~~~~~~~~~~~~~~
```

D. Use competency 5. Read the care label on the sweater. Read the sentences. Write *right* or *wrong*.

| Hand Wash in Cool Water Dry Flat |

1. Wash the sweater in a washing machine.   _____wrong_____

2. Use hot water to wash the sweater.   _____

3. Dry the sweater flat.   _____

Home

Unit Competencies

1. Talk about housing and neighborhoods
2. Read for-rent ads
3. Complete a change of address form
4. Read utility bills

What are the people doing? What are they saying? What do you think?

Practice the dialog.

➤ Our lease is almost up.
  It's a good time to think about moving.

● You're right. This apartment is too small.

➤ Let's look in today's paper.
  Maybe we can find something bigger.

● That's a good idea. Here's an interesting ad. Listen:
  "For rent. Two-bedroom house. Unfurnished. Small yard.
  Near City Park. $500 a month. Call 555–1801."

➤ That sounds pretty good. How much is the deposit?

● It's $200.

➤ Well, let's call about it.

Starting Out

A. Practice the dialogs.

➤ This house looks nice. And Carlota can play in the yard.

● It looks expensive.

➤ Well, we can call about it. What's the telephone number?

➤ Here's a three-bedroom apartment. It has lots of space.

● And there's a school nearby.

➤ Hmmm. It looks like there isn't any parking.

➤ A garage apartment would be all right.

● Sure. This neighborhood looks nice, too.

➤ But the apartment's furnished. We already have furniture.

➤ What about this mobile home? There are two bedrooms and two bathrooms.

● That would be nice. But is there a place for Carlota to play?

➤ No, there isn't.

B. Answer the questions.

1. Where do you think the people will move? Why?
2. Where would you move? Why?

Talk It Over

 A. Practice the dialog.

> ➤ Hello. Town Realty.
> ● Hello. This is **Joyce Chou.** I'm looking for **a house** to rent.
> ➤ We have **several houses** for rent. How many bedrooms do you want?
> ● **Two bedrooms and two bathrooms.**
> ➤ What neighborhood are you interested in?
> ● I'd like to be close to **City Elementary School.**
> ➤ Well, there are **a few houses for rent close to the school.**
>   Can you come by the office **at 2:00?**
> ● **Yes, I can be there this afternoon at 2:00.**

**B. You work at Town Realty. Talk to three students.
Where do they want to live? Use the dialog in A.
Write the answers.**

Name	Type of Housing	Number of Bedrooms	Number of Bathrooms	Close to
Joyce Chou	house	2	2	City Elementary School

Word Bank

A. Study the vocabulary.

furnished	lease	pet	**Appliances**
garage	mobile home	unfurnished	dishwasher
garage apartment	neighborhood	utilities	dryer
laundry	parking	yard	washer

B. Look at the picture. What kind of place is it? Write it down. Use words from A.

1. _____apartment_____   2. _____

3. _____   4. _____

C. Work with a partner.
Talk about a place you want to rent.
What appliances do you need?
What else do you want?

Listening

**A. Three people are calling about places to rent.
Look and listen. Number the homes.**

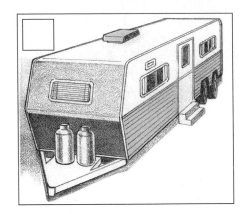

Rent _____ Deposit _____

Utilities:

___ gas ___ electricity ___ water

Are pets allowed? ___ yes ___ no

Rent __$315__ Deposit __$315__

Utilities:

___ gas ___ electricity ✔ water

Are pets allowed? ___ yes ✔ no

Rent _____ Deposit _____

Utilities:

___ gas ___ electricity ___ water

Are pets allowed? ___ yes ___ no

Listen again. Write the rent and the deposit.

**Listen again. Which utilities are included?
Are pets allowed?**

**B. Work in a small group. Talk about the places in A.
Where would you like to live?**

Reading

A. Read the rental ads.

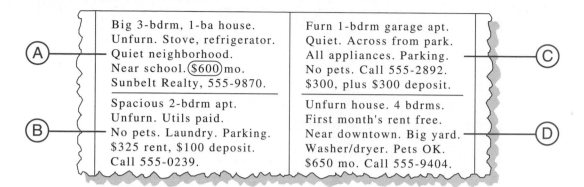

(A) Big 3-bdrm, 1-ba house.
Unfurn. Stove, refrigerator.
Quiet neighborhood.
Near school. $600 mo.
Sunbelt Realty, 555-9870.

(B) Spacious 2-bdrm apt.
Unfurn. Utils paid.
No pets. Laundry. Parking.
$325 rent, $100 deposit.
Call 555-0239.

(C) Furn 1-bdrm garage apt.
Quiet. Across from park.
All appliances. Parking.
No pets. Call 555-2892.
$300, plus $300 deposit.

(D) Unfurn house. 4 bdrms.
First month's rent free.
Near downtown. Big yard.
Washer/dryer. Pets OK.
$650 mo. Call 555-9404.

B. Read the words. Find the abbreviations that match. Write the letter of the answer.

   __c__   1. bedroom   a. apt

   _____   2. unfurnished   b. ba

   _____   3. bathroom   ✔ c. bdrm

   _____   4. apartment   d. furn

   _____   5. utilities   e. mo

   _____   6. furnished   f. unfurn

   _____   7. month   g. utils

C. Complete the exercise. Use the ads in A.

1. Circle the rent in each ad.
2. Joe is looking for a house.
   Which ads should he read? Write the letters. _____
3. Wendy is looking for a furnished apartment.
   What phone number should she call? _____
4. Federico wants to be close to the park.
   How many ads should he call about? _____
5. Nancy wants a washer and dryer.
   Should she call about the four-bedroom house? _____
6. Sara wants an apartment with parking.
   Which ads should she call about? Write the letters. _____

Structure Base

A. Study the examples.

There's a store	nearby.
	on the corner.
	around the corner.
	in the next block.
	three blocks away.
	across the street.
	down the street.

There's a store	next to	the building.
	close to	
	(not) far from	
	across the street from	
	down the street from	

B. The apartment manager at 1523 Pine Street is describing the neighborhood to Beth. Use the map. Use words from A to complete the sentences on page 93.

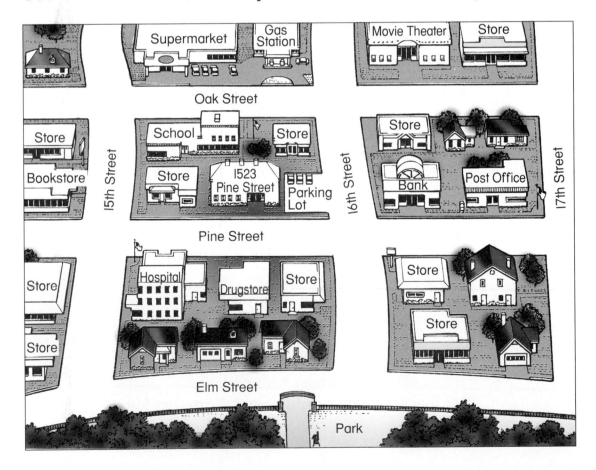

1. There's a **parking lot** _____next_____ to **the building.**

2. There's a **post office** _____ the street from **the building.**

3. There's a **school** around the _____ .

4. There's a **supermarket** in the next _____ .

5. There's a **park one block** _____ .

About You
C. Work with a partner.
Use the map to talk about the neighborhood.
What else can you say about it?

D. Study the examples.

Is there a store nearby?

Yes,	there	is.
No,		isn't.

E. Beth wants to know more about the neighborhood.
Use the map. Use words from D to complete the dialog.

➤ __Is there_____ a **movie theater** nearby?

● **Yes,** _____. There's a movie theater one block away.

➤ _____ a **laundromat** nearby?

● **No,** _____.

➤ _____ a **bookstore** nearby?

● **Yes,** _____. There's a bookstore in the next block.

About You
F. Work with a small group.
Talk about your neighborhoods.
Ask questions. Follow the examples in B and E.

Write It Down

A. You are moving on the first day of next month. You want the post office to send your mail to your new address. Complete the change of address form. Your new address is: 2003 Eighth Avenue, Apt. B Los Angeles, CA 90036.

U.S. Postal Service CHANGE OF ADDRESS ORDER	Customer Instructions: Complete Items 1 thru 9. Except Item 8, please PRINT all information including address on face of card.

1. Change of Address for *(Check one)*	☐ Individual	☐ Entire Family	☐ Business

2. Start Date	Month	Day	Year	3. If TEMPORARY address, print date to discontinue forwarding	Month	Day	Year

4. <u>Print</u> Last Name or Name of Business *(If more than one, use separate Change of Address Order Form for each).*

5. <u>Print</u> First Name of Head of Household *(include Jr., Sr., etc.).* Leave blank if the Change of Address Order is for a business.

6. <u>Print</u> OLD mailing address, number and street *(if Puerto Rico, include urbanization zone).*

Apt./Suite No.   P.O. Box No.

City   State   Zip Code

7. <u>Print</u> NEW mailing address, number and street

2 0 0 3   E i g h t h   A v e n u e

Apt./Suite No.   P.O. Box No.

City   State   Zip Code

8. Signature (See conditions on reverse).	OFFICIAL USE ONLY
9. Date signed Month Day Year	
OFFICIAL USE ONLY	
Verification Endorsement	

B. Work with a partner. Talk about the last time you moved. Did you use a change of address form? Why or why not? What happened?

C. Where would you like to live next? What kind of home would you look for? Write about three things you'd like in your home.

_____

_____

_____

1. Someone is calling Turner Realty.
Practice the dialog.

> ➤ Turner Realty. May I help you?
> ● Yes, I'm looking for a **two-bedroom house.**
> ➤ What neighborhood are you interested in?
> ● I want to be close to **an elementary school.**
> ➤ Well, we have a nice **two-bedroom house** for rent.
>   It's close to **Park Elementary School.**
> ● How much is the rent?
> ➤ It's **$400,** plus a **$300** deposit.
> ● I'd like to see it. What's the address?
> ➤ **4330 Kramer Lane.**

2. You're calling Turner Realty about an apartment.
Student B works there. Tell Student B what you want. Use
the dialog in I. Find out the rent, deposit, and address.

You want a 2-bedroom apartment. You want to be close to the park.

Rent: _____   Deposit: _____

Address: _____

3. You work for Turner Realty. Student B is calling
about a house. Use the ads. Follow the dialog in I.
Circle the house Student B would like.

2-bdrm house.	2-bdrm house.	1-bdrm house.
4330 Kramer Lane.	640 Spencer Street.	320 Larkin Street.
Near Park Elementary.	Near downtown.	Close to downtown.
Stove, refrigerator.	No pets. Washer/dryer.	Pets OK. Utils paid.
$400 mo rent.	$425 month.	Rent $380 mo.
$300 deposit.	One mo's rent deposit.	Deposit $200.

4. Switch roles. Turn to page 96. Complete 2 and 3.

5. Ask Student B about an apartment you'd like to rent.
Does Turner Realty have an apartment for you?

**I. Someone is calling Turner Realty.
    Practice the dialog.**

➤ Turner Realty. May I help you?

● Yes, I'm looking for a **two-bedroom house.**

➤ What neighborhood are you interested in?

● I want to be close to **an elementary school.**

➤ Well, we have a nice **two-bedroom house** for rent.
    It's close to **Park Elementary School.**

● How much is the rent?

➤ It's **$400,** plus a **$300** deposit.

● I'd like to see it. What's the address?

➤ **4330 Kramer Lane.**

**2. You work for Turner Realty. Student A is calling
    about an apartment. Use the ads. Follow the dialog in I.
    Circle the apartment Student A would like.**

33 Ivy Lane, Apt. 4. 1-bdrm apt. Stove, refrigerator. Small pets OK. $300 mo rent. $150 deposit.	2-bdrm apt. Close to County Park. 642 High Ave., Apt. 36. Stove, refrigerator. No pets. $350 mo, $250 deposit.	8401 First St., Apt. C. 3-bdrm apt. Close to downtown. No pets. Washer/dryer. $450 mo rent. $400 deposit.

**3. You're calling Turner Realty about a house.
    Student A works there. Tell Student A what you want. Use
    the dialog in I. Find out the rent, deposit, and address.**

You want a 1-bedroom house. You want to be close to downtown.

Rent: _____   Deposit: _____

Address: _____

4. Switch roles. Turn to page 95. Complete 2 and 3.

**5. Ask Student A about a house you'd like to rent.
    Does Turner Realty have a house for you?**

Extension

A. Thanh Ngo received this utility bill.
Look and read.

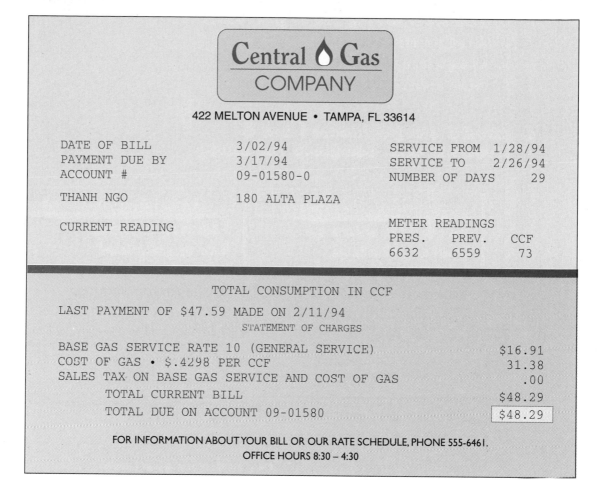

Central ⬥ Gas COMPANY

422 MELTON AVENUE • TAMPA, FL 33614

DATE OF BILL	3/02/94	SERVICE FROM	1/28/94
PAYMENT DUE BY	3/17/94	SERVICE TO	2/26/94
ACCOUNT #	09-01580-0	NUMBER OF DAYS	29

THANH NGO   180 ALTA PLAZA

CURRENT READING

METER READINGS

PRES.	PREV.	CCF
6632	6559	73

TOTAL CONSUMPTION IN CCF

LAST PAYMENT OF $47.59 MADE ON 2/11/94

STATEMENT OF CHARGES

BASE GAS SERVICE RATE 10 (GENERAL SERVICE)	$16.91
COST OF GAS • $.4298 PER CCF	31.38
SALES TAX ON BASE GAS SERVICE AND COST OF GAS	.00
TOTAL CURRENT BILL	$48.29
TOTAL DUE ON ACCOUNT 09-01580	$48.29

FOR INFORMATION ABOUT YOUR BILL OR OUR RATE SCHEDULE, PHONE 555-6461.
OFFICE HOURS 8:30 – 4:30

About You

B. Answer Thanh's questions about the bill.

1. What's the total? _____ $48.29

2. What's the due date? _____

3. What's the phone number of the gas company? _____

4. What are the office hours? _____

5. Where does Thanh send the payment?

_____

_____

_____

Check Your Competency

Can you use the competencies?

☐ 1. Talk about housing and neighborhoods
☐ 2. Read for-rent ads
☐ 3. Complete a change of address form
☐ 4. Read utility bills

A. Review competencies I and 2.
Read the ads. Complete the dialog.

FOR RENT	FOR RENT
Nice 2-bdrm unfurn apt.	3-bdrm furnished apt.
Quiet neighborhood.	Nice neighborhood.
Laundry. Small yard.	Close to City Elementary.
Utils paid. No pets.	Washer/dryer. Parking.
$500 rent, $300 deposit.	$575 rent + $500 deposit.
Call 555-3249.	Call 555-2829, evenings.

> **close to   neighborhood   rent   yard**

➤ Hello. I'm calling about the **two-bedroom apartment**

for _____rent_____.

● Yes. How can I help you?

➤ The ad says it's **in a quiet** _____.

Where is it?

● **Well, it's** _____ **City Park.**

There's a small _____.

➤ **That sounds good. When can I see it?**

Check
Up

Use competencies I and 2.
Use the dialog above to call about the other ad.

B. Use competency 3.
Complete the change of address form.
Your new address is: 573 Bonita Road, #2
Taos, NM 87571.

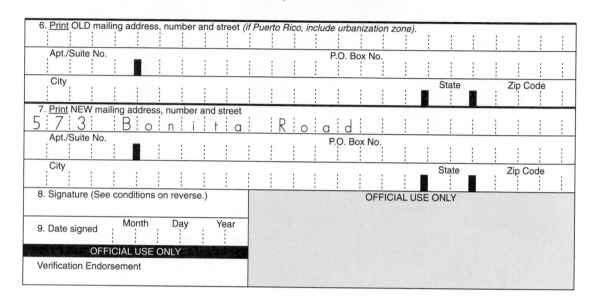

6. Print OLD mailing address, number and street *(if Puerto Rico, include urbanization zone)*.

| Apt./Suite No. | P.O. Box No. | | |
| City | | State | Zip Code |

7. Print NEW mailing address, number and street
5 7 3   B o n i t a   R o a d

| Apt./Suite No. | P.O. Box No. | | |
| City | | State | Zip Code |

8. Signature (See conditions on reverse.)   OFFICIAL USE ONLY

9. Date signed   Month   Day   Year

OFFICIAL USE ONLY

Verification Endorsement

C. Use competency 4. Read the utility bill.
Answer the questions. Write the letter of the answer.

Southern Electric Company
P.O. BOX 359, GREENVILLE, SC 29615

KIM LEE
361 BIRCHWOOD AVE., #13
GREENVILLE, SC 29615

METER READ: 4 | 20 | 94
KILOWATTS USED: 149

TOTAL DUE: $ 22.50
PAYMENT DUE: 5 | 4 | 94

Call 555-4431 with questions about your bill.
Office hours, Monday to Friday, 9:00 – 5:00

<u>b</u> 1. What's the customer's name?   a. $22.50

_____ 2. What's the total?   ✔ b. Kim Lee

_____ 3. What's the due date?   c. 555–4431

_____ 4. What's the phone number   d. 5/4/94
of the electric company?

What are the people doing? What are they saying? What do you think?

Practice the dialog.

➤ Hey, Felipe. Are you all right?

● No. I feel sick.

➤ You don't look well. And you sound terrible.

● I think I have a fever. I'm coughing and sneezing.
I have a headache, too. I really need to see a doctor.
Do you know a good one?

➤ Yes, I do. I like my doctor a lot. Her name's Sara Levy.

● What's her phone number?

➤ I don't have it with me, but she's in the phone book.

● Dr. Sara Levy. Thanks.

Starting Out

 A. Practice the dialogs.

➤ Diane doesn't feel well.
I think she has a fever.

● Take her temperature.
If she has a fever, you should
call your pediatrician.

➤ I think I have the flu.
But I don't know if I should
take any medicine.

● Well, Kim, I think you should
call your obstetrician first.

➤ Nico's teacher says he can't
read the board at school.

● If he has trouble seeing, take
him to an eye doctor.
Maybe he needs new glasses.

➤ My daughter Hu-lan has a
little cough.

● Maybe she should take some
cough medicine.

➤ What kind should I buy?

 B. Answer the questions.

1. Which people need to see doctors?
2. When do you take medicine? When do you see a doctor?
What kind of doctor do you usually see?

Talk It Over

A. Practice the dialog.

➤ What's the matter?
● I have a **backache.**
➤ Maybe you should **take some aspirin.**

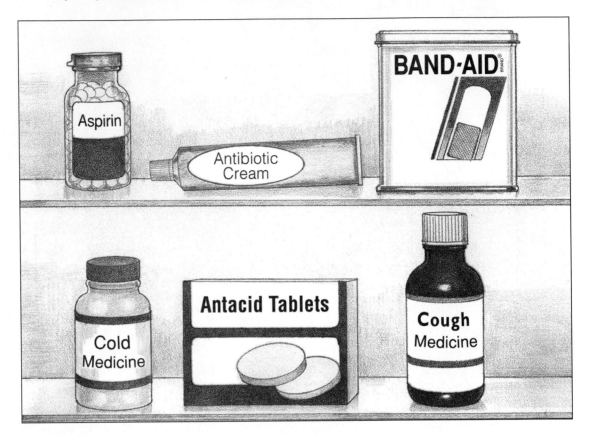

**B. Work with a partner. Look at the medicine.
Use the dialog in A to talk about these health problems.**

1. You have a headache.
2. You have a cold.
3. You have a cough.
4. You have a cut on your finger.
5. You have a stomachache.

**C. Work with a partner. Talk about other health problems.
What medicine should people take for them?**

Word Bank

A. Study the vocabulary.

Doctors
eye doctor
obstetrician
pediatrician

Useful Language
I think you should (see a doctor).
Have you ever had (surgery)?

Medicine
antacid
antibiotic (cream)
aspirin
Band-Aids®
caution
cold medicine
cough medicine
drowsiness

pill
prescription
refill

allergic
allergies
asthma
cancer

diabetes
heart attack
high blood pressure
pregnant
sneeze
surgery
tuberculosis

B. Complete the sentences. Use words from A.

1. My sister's pregnant. She's looking for

   a good _____ obstetrician _____.

2. Her son had a cough, so she gave him

   some cough _____.

3. Her son's cough isn't better, so she's taking him

   to the _____.

4. The doctor is giving her a _____ for medicine

   for her son.

C. Work with a partner. Use words from A. Talk about medicine you have at home. When do you take the medicine?

Listening

**A. Look and listen. Three people are seeing doctors.
Circle the doctors they're seeing in column A.**

A	B	C
1. eye doctor (obstetrician) pediatrician	backache stomachache (cold)	Take some antacid. Take some aspirin. (Don't take any aspirin.)
2. eye doctor obstetrician pediatrician	headache trouble seeing sore throat	Take an eye test. Take some aspirin. Get plenty of sleep.
3. eye doctor obstetrician pediatrician	cough earache stomachache	Take him to another doctor. Give him some medicine. Don't take any aspirin.

**Listen again. What's the matter with the people?
Circle the answer in column B.**

**Listen again. What do the doctors say to do?
Circle the answer in column C.**

**B. Work with a partner.
Talk about other doctors you know about.**

Unit 8

Reading

A. This is a health questionnaire.
   It can help you improve your health habits.
   Answer the questions. Then add up your points.

How Healthy Are You?

Read the questions. Circle your answers.
Then circle your points.

1. **How long do you sleep each day?**
   a. More than 7 hours   2 points
   b. 5-7 hours   1 point
   c. Less than 5 hours   0 points

2. **How much do you exercise each week?**
   a. More than 2 times   2 points
   b. 1-2 times   1 point
   c. Never   0 points

3. **How many glasses of water do you drink each day?**
   a. More than 4   2 points
   b. 2-4   1 point
   c. 0-1   0 points

4. **How often do you eat fried foods?**
   a. Never   2 points
   b. 1-3 times a week   1 point
   c. More than 3 times a week   0 points

5. **How often do you have candy, dessert, soda pop, or other food with sugar?**
   a. 0-1 times a week   2 points
   b. 2-3 times a week   1 point
   c. More than 3 times a week   0 points

6. **How many times do you brush your teeth each day?**
   a. 3 times or more   2 points
   b. 2 times   1 point
   c. 1 time   0 points

**Add your points.
Then find your total.**

9-12 points
Congratulations! If you keep doing what you are doing now, you should stay healthy.

5-8 points
Pretty good. You should look at the questions with low scores. What can you do to get more points?

0-4 points
Oh, no! If this is your total, you should look for ways to get more points. Then make some changes—you can be healthy, too!

YOU AND YOUR HEALTH

**B. Write three good health habits you have.
Write three things you can do to be healthier.**

Structure Base

A. Study the examples.

| You | should
shouldn't | take aspirin. |

B. What should you do to be healthy?
Complete the sentences with *should* or *shouldn't*.

1. You _____should get_____ (get) plenty of rest.

2. You _____ (get) exercise.

3. You _____ (eat) food with a lot of sugar.

4. You _____ (drink) plenty of water.

5. You _____ (eat) fried foods.

6. You _____ (eat) vegetables.

C. What can Bob do to be healthier?
Write sentences with *should* and *shouldn't*.

_____

_____

_____

D. Study the examples.

> If you have a headache, (you should) take some aspirin.
> (You should) take some aspirin if you have a headache.

E. Complete the sentences.
Write the letter of the answer.

1. If the baby is sick, __c__ .

2. If you have a toothache, _____ .

3. If you have a cough, _____ .

4. If you have trouble seeing, _____ .

a. take some cough medicine
b. you should go to an eye doctor
✔ c. take her to a pediatrician
d. you shouldn't eat sugar

F. Complete the sentences.

1. If you're sick, _____you should see a doctor_____ .

2. You should take some aspirin if _____

_____ .

3. You should see a doctor if _____

_____ .

4. If you're allergic to medicine, _____

_____ .

5. If you're pregnant, _____

_____ .

6. If you have a stomachache, _____

_____ .

7. If you have a cut, _____

_____ .

Write It Down

**You have an appointment with a new doctor.
The doctor needs to know your medical history.
Complete the form.**

MEDICAL HISTORY

Patient's Name _____
                 Last   First

Address _____
         Street

_____
     City   State   ZIP Code

Phone (home) _____ (work) _____

Date of Birth _____

When was your last check-up? _____

Put a check (✔) by problems you have had.

____ allergies	____ diabetes	____ high blood pressure
____ asthma	____ headaches	____ tuberculosis
____ cancer	____ heart attack	

Answer the questions. Write *yes* or *no*.

1. Are you allergic to any medicine? If yes, what kind?

_____

2. Did you ever stay in the hospital? If yes, what for?

_____

3. Are you taking any medicine now? If yes, what kind?

_____

4. Do you have insurance? If yes, what is the name of the insurance company?

_____

1. Practice the dialog.

➤ **Mary** has a **headache**.

● If **she** has a **headache, she** should **take some aspirin.**

 2. What's the matter with the people? Tell Student B. Follow the dialog in 1. Write what the people should do.

 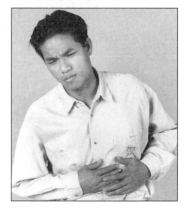 

a. Mary   b. Nam   c. Amparo

take some aspirin   _____   _____

_____   _____   _____

 3. Student B knows some people who are sick. Look at the medicine. Follow the dialog in 1. Tell Student B what the people should do.

4. Switch roles. Turn to page 110. Complete 2 and 3.

One To One

I. Practice the dialog.

> ➤ **Mary** has a **headache.**
>
> ● If **she** has a **headache, she** should **take some aspirin.**

2. Student A knows some people who are sick. Look at the medicine. Follow the dialog in I. Tell Student A what the people should do.

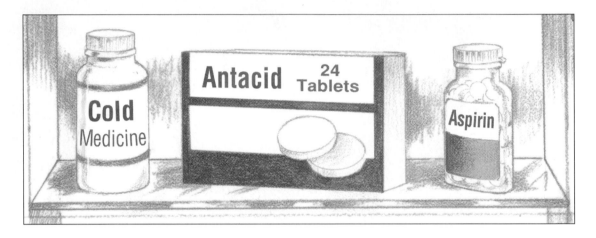

3. What's the matter with the people? Tell Student A. Follow the dialog in I. Write what the people should do.

a. Benito   b. Li-ming   c. Mike

_____   _____   _____

_____   _____   _____

4. Switch roles. Turn to page 109. Complete 2 and 3.

Unit 8

Extension

A. It's important to follow the directions on medicine labels. Read the label on the prescription medicine.

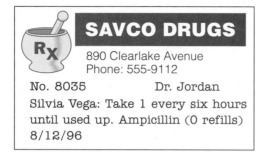

SAVCO DRUGS

890 Clearlake Avenue
Phone: 555-9112

No. 8035   Dr. Jordan

Silvia Vega: Take 1 every six hours
until used up. Ampicillin (0 refills)
8/12/96

 About You

B. Read the sentences about the prescription label. Write *yes* or *no*.

1. The medicine is for Silvia Vega.   <u>   yes   </u>

2. She should take one pill every four hours.   _____

3. The name of the medicine is Ampicillin.   _____

C. Read the label on the non-prescription medicine.

Quiet **COUGH** MEDICINE

For relief of coughs
and minor sore throat.
To help you get the
"Quiet" you need.

4.5 fluid ounces

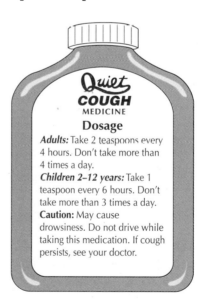

Quiet **COUGH** MEDICINE

Dosage

Adults: Take 2 teaspoons every
4 hours. Don't take more than
4 times a day.
Children 2–12 years: Take 1
teaspoon every 6 hours. Don't
take more than 3 times a day.
Caution: May cause
drowsiness. Do not drive while
taking this medication. If cough
persists, see your doctor.

 About You

D. Answer the questions.

1. What kind of medicine is it? <u> cough medicine </u>

2. If Lydia is one year old, should she take this medicine? _____

3. If David takes this medicine, should he drive? _____

Check Your Competency

Can you use the competencies?

☐ 1. Identify kinds of doctors
☐ 2. Talk about symptoms and medicine
☐ 3. Identify practices that lead to good health
☐ 4. Read medicine labels
☐ 5. Complete medical history forms
☐ 6. Listen to doctors' advice

A. Use competency 1. Read about Daniel and his family. What kinds of doctors should they see? Write the letter.

_c_   1. Daniel needs glasses.   a. obstetrician

_____ 2. His sister is pregnant.   b. pediatrician

_____ 3. His baby needs a check-up. ✔ c. eye doctor

B. Review competency 2. Complete the dialog.

✔

aspirin sick feel fever

➤ Hi, **Gina.** Hey, do you _____feel_____ OK?

● Well, no, I don't. **I think I'm** _____.

   I have a 100 degree _____ and my head aches.

➤ Maybe you should take some _____.

● You're right. I'm going to take some right now.

Use competency 2. Use the dialog above to talk about health problems and medicine.

C. Use competency 3. Circle the good health habits.

(Get plenty of sleep.)   Eat lots of food with sugar.

Watch plenty of TV.   Get exercise.

Drink plenty of water.   Eat fresh fruit and vegetables.

D. Use competency 4.
Read the medicine label.
Answer the questions.

COMPLETE COLD MEDICINE

Dosage: *Adults* *(Ages 14 and up):* 2 pills every 6 hours.

Children *(Ages 6-14):* 1 pill every 8 hours.

Caution: May cause drowsiness.
Do not drive while taking this medication.

1. What is this medicine for? ___a cold___

2. How many pills should an adult take? _____

3. Tom is ten years old. How many pills should he take? _____

4. If you take this medicine, should you drive? _____

E. Use competency 5. Complete the medical history form.

MEDICAL HISTORY
PUT A CHECK (✔) BY PROBLEMS YOU HAVE HAD.

_____ allergies   _____ cancer   _____ heart attack

_____ asthma   _____ headaches   _____ tuberculosis

Answer the questions. Write *yes* **or** *no.*
1. Are you allergic to any medicine? If yes, what kind?

_____

2. Are you taking any medicine now? If yes, what kind?

_____

F. Use competency 6. Look and listen.
What does the doctor tell the patient? Circle the answers.

Take some antacid.

Take some cough medicine.

Take some aspirin.

Employment

Unit Competencies

1. Ask about job openings
2. Interview for a job
3. Accept a job offer
4. Complete a Social Security form
5. Listen to instructions at work
6. Explain absences from work

What are the people doing? What are they saying? What do you think?

Practice the dialog.

> Hello. I'm Elena Canales.
> Do you have any openings for electronics assemblers?

● Yes. We have one opening. Do you have any experience?

> Yes. I worked at Computech for two years.

● Why did you leave?

> The company closed.

● All right. Fill out this application.
  We'll let you know something next week.

Starting Out

A. Practice the dialog.

➤ Hello.

● Hello, **Ms. Canales.** I'm calling about the **electronics assembler** job. Are you still interested?

➤ Yes, I am.

● Good. Which shift do you prefer—first or second?

➤ **I like to spend the evenings with my children, so I'd prefer the first shift.**

● And do you want to work part time or full time?

➤ **Full time.**

● When can you start?

➤ **Immediately.**

● Well, how's **next Monday?**

➤ **Next Monday** would be fine. Thank you.

B. Work with a partner. You applied for a job last week. Use the dialog in A to give the employer more information about yourself.

Talk It Over

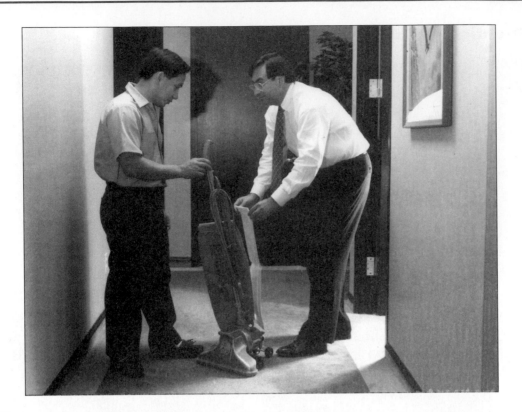

 A. Hoan just started a new job. He's a custodian. Practice the dialog.

> ➤ Hoan, please vacuum the offices today. Don't forget to change the bag on the vacuum cleaner first.
> ● Excuse me, Mr. Delgado. Could you show me how?
> ➤ Of course. Open the top, pull out the bag, and put in a new one.
> ● Let me try. Is this right?
> ➤ Yes. Please empty the trash cans and change the light bulb in the main office, too.
> ● I'm sorry. Could you repeat that, please?
> ➤ Sure. Empty the trash cans and change the light bulb in the main office.
> ● OK. Now I've got it. Thanks.

B. Answer the questions.

1. What does Mr. Delgado ask Hoan to do?
2. What kinds of questions does Hoan ask? Why does he ask them?

C. Work with a partner. Talk about work. Take turns being employer and employee. Use the dialog in A. Give each other instructions.

Word Bank

A. Study the vocabulary.

application	interview	carpenter	housekeeper
employee	opening	custodian	waiter/
employer	part time	dishwasher	waitress
experience	shift	electronics	
full time		assembler	

B. Look at the pictures. Use words from A. Write the jobs.

1. _electronics assembler_

2. _____

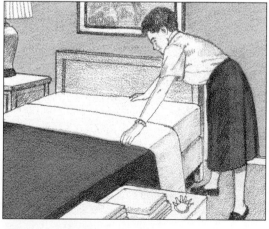

3. _____

4. _____

About You

C. Work with a partner. Talk about a job you want. Do you want to work part time or full time? Can you work on weekends? When can you start?

Listening

A. Three people are at job interviews. Look and listen. Circle the jobs they want in column A.

A	B
1. dishwasher electronics assembler	six months six years
2. carpenter custodian	three years five years
3. housekeeper cashier	no experience four years

Listen again. How much experience do they have? Circle the answer in column B.

B. It's Shelly's first day of work as a housekeeper. What does she have to do? Circle the instructions.

Clean the sink, the toilet, and the tub.   Wash the windows.

Put towels and soap in the bathroom.   Water the plants.

Wash the dishes.   Empty the trash cans.

Make the beds.   Vacuum the room.

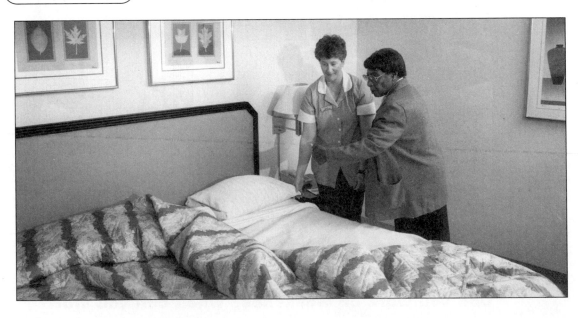

Reading

A. Look and read.

INTERVIEWS
How to Get the Job You Want

Usually the first time an employer sees you is at the job interview. What can you do to look and sound right for the job?

First you need to look your best. Make sure your hair and your clothes are clean and neat.

Next arrive at the job interview five or ten minutes early so an employer knows you can be on time. It's a good idea to bring your Social Security card with you. And bring a pen, so you can complete a job application.

During the interview, answer the employer's questions clearly. Tell the employer about your experience. If you don't have experience, tell the employer that you want to learn. You can ask the employer polite questions about the job, too. Don't chew gum, smoke, or drink coffee during the interview.

Always thank the employer for the interview. And remember—even if you don't get the job, you are getting good practice for your next interview. If you know how to interview, you can get the job you want! ◆

B. Read the sentences about job interviews. Write *yes* or *no*.

yes   1. It's important to look clean and neat for a job interview.

_____   2. It's OK to be five or ten minutes late for the interview.

_____   3. You should take your Social Security card to the interview.

_____   4. It's OK to drink coffee during the interview.

_____   5. You can ask questions about the job.

_____   6. You should thank the employer for the interview.

C. Work with a small group. Answer the questions.

1. What are some good reasons to go to an interview early?
2. What are some things you should and shouldn't do at an interview?
3. Think of more ways to do well at a job interview. Make a list.

Structure Base

A. Study the examples.

Could you	repeat that, please?
	show me how?

B. Tamara has a new job as a dishwasher. Her employer is explaining the job. Complete the dialog. Use the words from A.

➤ First take all the food off the dishes and put the dishes

in the dishwasher.

● <u>Could you show</u> (show) me where to put the food?

➤ Here, in this trash can. Then run the dishwasher.

● _____ (tell) me how to run it?

➤ Sure. Add the soap, close the door, and push these buttons.

● I'm sorry. _____ (repeat) that, please?

➤ Of course. Add the soap, close the door, and push these buttons.

And _____ (clean) the sink after you finish?

● Yes, of course.

➤ OK. Thank you.

C. Work with a partner. Take turns telling how to do a job. Use the examples in A and B to ask questions with *could.*

D. Study the examples.

<u>I'm looking for a job because I want to learn new skills.</u>
I want to learn new skills, so I'm looking for a job.

One To One

I. Practice the dialog.

> ➤ Hello. I'd like to apply for the **cook** position.
> ● Do you have any experience as a **cook?**
> ➤ Yes. I worked as a **cook** for **two years.**
>   I was a **dishwasher** for **one year** before that.
> ● When can you start?
> ➤ **In two weeks.**

2. You want a job. Student B is an employer.
Use the application form to answer Student B's questions.
Follow the dialog in I.

Application For Employment		

Position applied for? ___cook___

When can you start? ___in two weeks___

EXPERIENCE

Position	Place of Business	Length of Employment
cook	Franco's Restaurant	2 years
dishwasher	Ron's Diner	1 year

3. You are an employer. Student B wants a job.
Follow the dialog in I. Complete the information.

Position: ___custodian___

Experience: ___2 years as a custodian___

___ as a ___

When can this person start? ___

4. Switch roles. Turn to page 124. Complete 2 and 3.

One To One

I. Practice the dialog.

➤ Hello. I'd like to apply for the **cook** position.

● Do you have any experience as a **cook?**

➤ Yes. I worked as a **cook** for **two years.**
I was a **dishwasher** for **one year** before that.

● When can you start?

➤ **In two weeks.**

2. You are an employer. Student A wants a job.
Follow the dialog in I. Complete the information.

Position: _____cook_____

Experience: _2 years as a cook_____

_____as a_____

When can this person start? _____

3. You want a job. Student A is an employer.
Use the application form to answer Student A's questions.
Follow the dialog in I.

Application For Employment		
Position applied for? _custodian_____		
When can you start? _immediately_____		
EXPERIENCE		
Position	Place of Business	Length of Employment
custodian	Computech	2 years
housekeeper	people's homes	5 years

4. Switch roles. Turn to page 123. Complete 2 and 3.

Extension

 A. Practice the dialog.

> ➤ Hello. This is **Tony.** I'm sorry, but I'm going to **be late for** work today. I'm **having car trouble.**
> ● When do you think you can be here?
> ➤ **I'm not sure. I think I can be there this afternoon.**
> ● All right, **Tony.** Thanks for the call.

B. Sometimes you have to miss work.
Here are three good reasons you can't be at work.

1. You're sick.
2. You have a doctor's appointment.
3. You have car trouble.

Work in a small group.
Write two more good reasons you can't be at work.

_____

_____

C. Work with a partner. Use the dialog in A.
Call about a good reason you can't be at work.

Can you use the competencies?

- ☐ 1. Ask about job openings
- ☐ 2. Interview for a job
- ☐ 3. Accept a job offer
- ☐ 4. Complete a Social Security form
- ☐ 5. Listen to instructions at work
- ☐ 6. Explain absences from work

A. Review competencies l, 2, and 3. Complete the dialog.

| experience | openings | start | thank | waitress |

➤ I want a job as **a waitress.** Do you have any ___openings___?

● Yes, we do. Do you have any _____ as **a waitress?**

➤ **Yes, I worked as a** _____ **for one year**

at Chen's Restaurant.

● When can you _____?

➤ **Immediately.**

● OK. How about **Tuesday evening at 6:00?**

● **That's fine.** _____ **you.**

Use competencies l, 2, and 3.
Use the dialog above to apply for a job you want.

B. Use competency 4.
Complete the form to apply for a Social Security number.

SOCIAL SECURITY ADMINISTRATION
Application for a Social Security Card

NAME _____

       FIRST   FULL MIDDLE NAME   LAST

CITIZENSHIP
Check one. (✔)

☐ U.S. Citizen   ☐ Legal Alien Allowed to Work   ☐ Legal Alien Not Allowed to Work

☐ Foreign Student Allowed Restricted Employment   ☐ Conditionally Legalized Alien Allowed to Work   ☐ Other

---

SEX   ☐ Male   ☐ Female

DATE OF BIRTH   **PLACE OF BIRTH**

_____   _____

MONTH / DAY / YEAR   CITY   STATE OR FOREIGN COUNTRY

C. Use competency 5. Listen. It's Ernesto's first day as a custodian. What does Ernesto have to do?
Circle the answers.

Wash the windows.   Clean the bathrooms.

Empty the trash cans.   (Vacuum the offices.)

Change the light bulbs.   Clean the desks.

D. Review competency 6. Complete the dialog.

✔

call   sick   sorry   work

➤ Hello. This is **Anne Kane.** I'm _____sorry_____, but I can't

come to _____ today. **I'm** _____.

● **I'm sorry you're sick, Anne.** Thanks for the _____.

Use competency 6. Use the dialog above.
Call about a good reason you can't be at work.

Transportation and Travel

Unit Competencies

1. Talk about getting a driver's license
2. Identify safe driving practices
3. Identify car maintenance procedures
4. Ask for and give road directions
5. Read road maps

What are the people doing? What are they saying? What do you think?

Practice the dialog.

➤ Hi, Maria. What are you doing?

● Hi, Martin. I'm looking for a used car in the want ads.

➤ That's a good way to find a car. You probably should go to a few used car dealers, too.

● Good idea. Any other suggestions?

➤ You should test drive a car before you buy it. And get a mechanic to check under the hood. By the way, do you have a U.S. driver's license?

● No. My license is from Mexico.

➤ Well, you know you have to get a license before you can drive here.

● Yes. I'm taking the test next week.

Starting Out

 A. This is how Maria got her driver's license.
Look and read.

1. First Maria had to fill out an application and take a vision test.

2. Then Maria took the written test. She studied for the test, so she passed easily.

3. Maria got her learner's permit. Every day she drove with a licensed driver.

4. Finally Maria took the driving test. She did well, and she got her license.

 B. Answer the questions.

1. What did Maria do to get her driver's license?
2. Do you have a driver's license? What did you have to do to get it?

Talk It Over

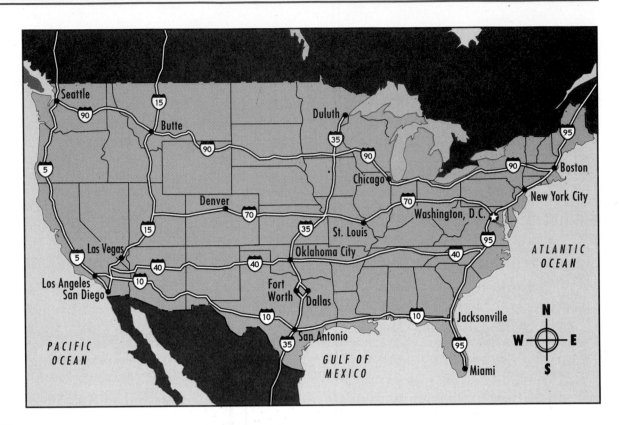

 A. Curtis and Park live in San Antonio, Texas.
Curtis is planning a car trip.
Look at the map. Practice the dialog.

➤ Do you know how to get from **here** to **Los Angeles?**
● Sure. **Take Interstate 10 west all the way.**
➤ That sounds easy to follow.
● It is, but it's a long trip.

B. Work with a partner. Use the map. Use the dialog in A.
Talk about going from Washington, D.C., to Miami, Florida.

C. Look at the map. Where do you want to go?
Where does your partner want to go?
Use the dialog in A to ask for and give directions.

Word Bank

A. Study the vocabulary.

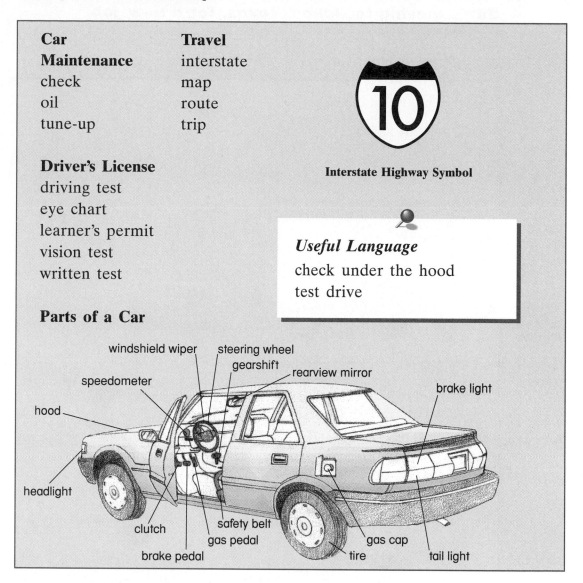

Car Maintenance
check
oil
tune-up

Travel
interstate
map
route
trip

Interstate Highway Symbol

Driver's License
driving test
eye chart
learner's permit
vision test
written test

Useful Language
check under the hood
test drive

Parts of a Car

windshield wiper
steering wheel
gearshift
rearview mirror
speedometer
brake light
hood
headlight
clutch
safety belt
gas pedal
brake pedal
tire
gas cap
tail light

B. Complete the sentences. Use words from A.

1. To steer the car, use the _____steering wheel_____.

2. To stop the car, use the _____.

3. To see behind the car, use the _____.

4. To see how fast you're going, look at the _____.

 **C. Work with a small group. Talk about travel.
Where do you go? Do you drive or take public
transportation? Do you ever use a map?**

Listening

A. Emily lives in Chicago, Illinois.
She's moving to Dallas, Texas, for a new job.
Work with a partner. Look at the map.
Find three routes Emily can take.

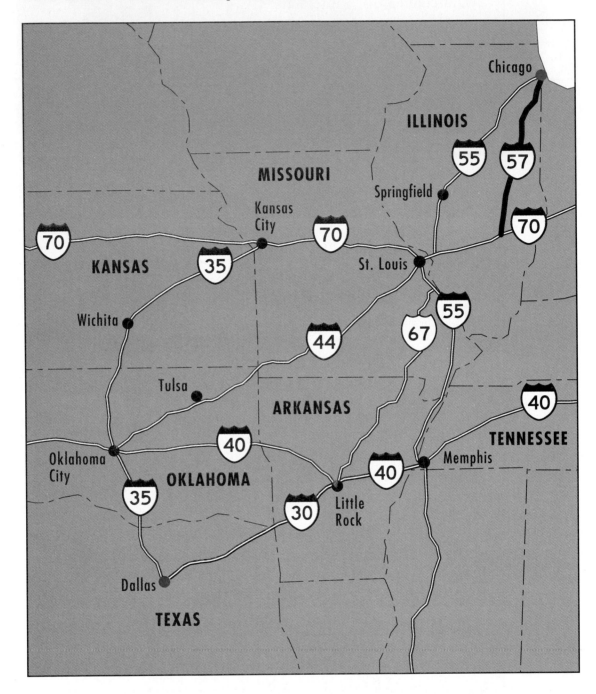

 B. Emily is asking a friend for directions to Dallas from Chicago. Listen. Mark the route on the map.

 C. Work with a small group. Talk about the map. Which route would you take from Chicago to Dallas? Why?

Reading

A. Read the article.

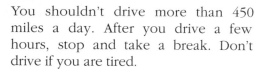

Plan Your Car Trip
Car trips can be a lot of fun if you plan them carefully.

✓ Make sure your car is in good shape.
✓ Check the oil, water, and tires before leaving.
✓ Take the name and telephone number of your insurance company with you.

You shouldn't drive more than 450 miles a day. After you drive a few hours, stop and take a break. Don't drive if you are tired.

During the trip, check the gas indicator often. You shouldn't let the gas get too low.

Take healthful snack food, such as fruit, popcorn, or nuts, to eat along the way. And take something to drink. If you are driving with children, stop frequently.

Let them get out of the car and stretch their legs.

It's always a good idea to have a first-aid kit in your car. If you drive in the winter in snow or ice, you should use snow tires or chains. Also, take a blanket along, in case of an emergency.

Tell relatives or friends where you plan to be each night. This way, if there's an emergency, they can find you. Think ahead. Plan carefully. Then enjoy your trip! ◆

B. Beatrice and Marco want to take a car trip. This is what they're going to do. Write *right* or *wrong*.

1. They're going to check the car before they leave. ___right___

2. They're going to drive 650 miles the first day. _____

3. They aren't taking anything to eat. _____

4. They're taking a first-aid kit with them. _____

5. They're not telling anyone their plans. _____

C. What are Beatrice and Marco doing wrong? Write what they should do.

They should drive no more than 450 miles a day.

_____

_____

Structure Base

A. Study the examples.

I	should make sure my car is in good shape.
	shouldn't drive more than 450 miles a day.

B. You are planning a car trip. What should you do? Complete the sentences. Follow the examples in A.

1. You _____should check_____ **(check)** the oil, water, and tires.

2. You _____ **(stop)** after a few hours and take a break.

3. You _____ **(drive)** if you're too tired.

4. You _____ **(take)** healthful snack food along.

C. Study the examples.

What	do	I	have to do?
	does	she	

I	have to	get a driver's license.
She	has to	

D. Complete the dialog. Follow the examples in C.

➤ I _____have to get_____ **(get)** a driver's license.

   What _do_ I _____have to do_____ **(do)**?

● First you _____ **(complete)** an application.

➤ What _____ I _____ **(do)** next?

● Well, you _____ **(pass)** the vision test.

➤ OK. What else _____ I _____ **(do)**?

● You _____ **(pass)** a written test and a driving test.

E. Study the examples.

> If you drive in the winter, (you should) put snow tires on your car.
> (You should) put snow tires on your car if you drive in the winter.

F. Complete the sentences. Write the letter.

1. If you drive in the rain, __c__.

2. If you want to take a car trip, _____.

3. If you are driving with children, _____.

4. You should use the rearview mirror _____.

a. if you want to see behind your car
b. you should plan your trip carefully
✔ c. you should use the windshield wipers
d. stop frequently and let them get out of the car

G. Study the examples.

> Maria passed the written test easily because she studied for it.
> Maria studied for the written test, so she passed it easily.

H. Complete the sentences. Use words from G.

1. I need to get a U.S. driver's license ____because____ mine is from Mexico.

2. I studied for the written test _____ I wanted to do well.

3. I could read the eye chart, _____ I passed the vision test.

4. I got my learner's permit _____ I passed the written test, too.

5. I practiced driving every day, _____ I passed the driving test.

Write It Down

**A. Martina is planning a party for her friends.
Here's a map and directions to her house.
Look at the map. Complete the directions.**

Interstate 23

To Middletown

Interstate 17

To Mountainview

Washington Street

N
W E
S

My House
122 Washington Street

To Downtown

Fourth Avenue

If you live in Middletown, take _____Interstate 23_____

east to Washington Street. Go south on

_____ . I'm at 122 Washington Street.

If you live in Mountainview, take _____

south to _____ . Go_____ on Fourth

Avenue to Washington Street. Go north on

_____ until you get to 122.

If you're coming from downtown, go west on

_____ to Washington Street.

Go _____ on Washington Street until you get to 122.

**B. You want to have a party.
On a sheet of paper, draw a map to your house.
Write directions.**

One To One

I. Practice the dialog.

➤ How do I get from **Los Angeles, California,** to **San Diego, California?**

● Take **Interstate 5 south.**

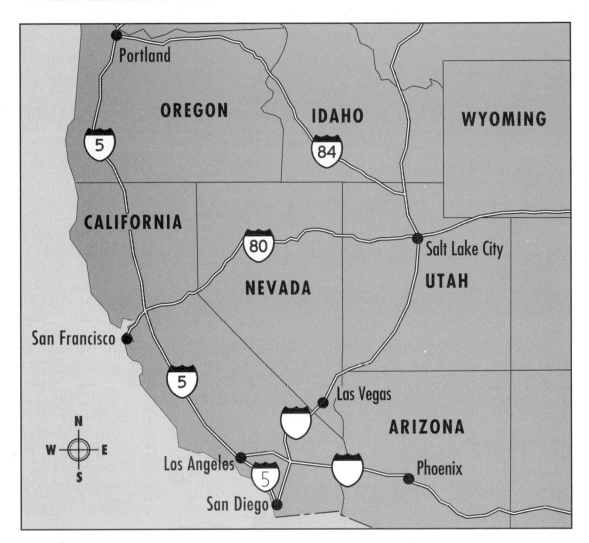

 2. You're in Los Angeles, California. Ask Student B for directions to these cities. Follow the dialog in I. Find the routes and write the interstate numbers on the map.

a. San Diego, California

b. Phoenix, Arizona

c. Las Vegas, Nevada

 3. Student B is in San Francisco, California, and needs directions. Use the map. Follow the dialog in I. Give Student B directions.

One To One

I. Practice the dialog.

➤ How do I get from **Los Angeles, California,** to
San Diego, California?

● Take **Interstate 5 south.**

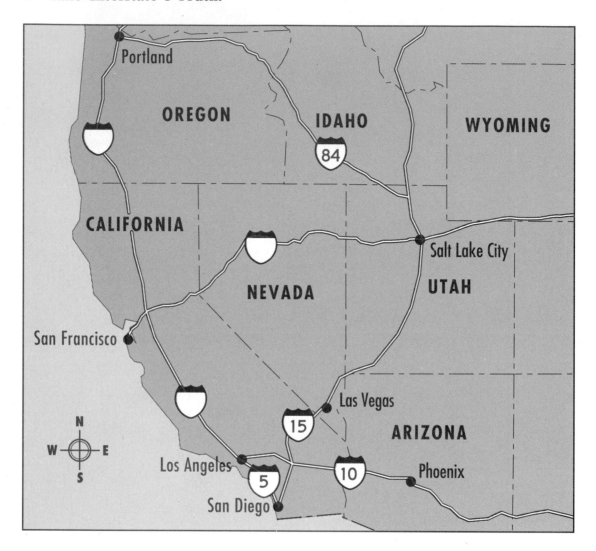

**2. Student A is in Los Angeles, California, and needs
directions. Use the map. Follow the dialog in I.
Give Student A directions.**

**3. You're in San Francisco, California. Ask Student A for
directions to these cities. Follow the dialog in I. Find the
routes and mark the interstate numbers on the map.**

a. Salt Lake City, Utah
b. Portland, Oregon
c. Los Angeles, California

Extension

A. Look and read.

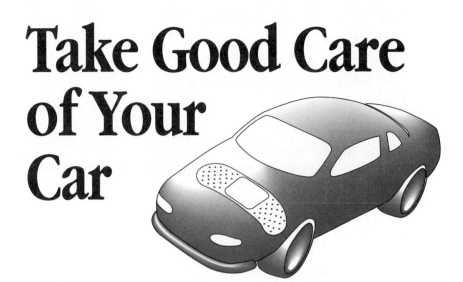

Take Good Care of Your Car

The best way to keep your car running well is to do regular car maintenance. Regular maintenance helps your car stay dependable and safe. Here is a list of things everyone should do.

- ☐ 1. Change the oil and check the water every three months.
- ☐ 2. Get a tune-up once a year.
- ☐ 3. Make sure the headlights, tail lights, and brake lights all work.
- ☐ 4. Check the tires regularly. Make sure there's enough air in them.

New cars come with manuals that give specific information on how to take care of the cars. If you have a used car and you don't have a manual, look in the library for books on how to take care of your car.

Remember—regular maintenance is the key to a safe, dependable car. If you take good care of your car, it will take good care of you.

B. Answer the questions.

1. Why is regular car maintenance important?
2. What information can you find in a car manual?

About You **C. Work in a small group. Talk about things all car drivers should check.**

Check Your Competency

Can you use the competencies?

- ☐ 1. Talk about getting a driver's license
- ☐ 2. Identify safe driving practices
- ☐ 3. Identify car maintenance procedures
- ☐ 4. Ask for and give road directions
- ☐ 5. Read road maps

A. Use competency 1.
Circle the steps in getting a driver's license.

Test drive the cars.　　Read ads in the paper.

(Take a vision test.)　　Go to a few car dealers.

Take a written test.　　Take a driving test.

B. Use competency 2. You want to take a car trip.
What should you do? Read the sentences.
Write *right* or *wrong*.

1. Plan the trip carefully.　　_____right_____

2. Don't drive if you're too tired.　　_____

3. Don't take anything to eat or drink.　　_____

4. Take a first-aid kit.　　_____

5. Don't tell anyone where you're going.　　_____

C. Use competency 3. Read the sentences.
Circle the regular car maintenance procedures.

(Check the oil and water.)　　Get a learner's permit.

Get a tune-up.　　Check the tires.

Check a map.　　Check the battery.

D. Review competencies 4 and 5. Look at the map. Complete the dialog. Write the number of the interstate highway.

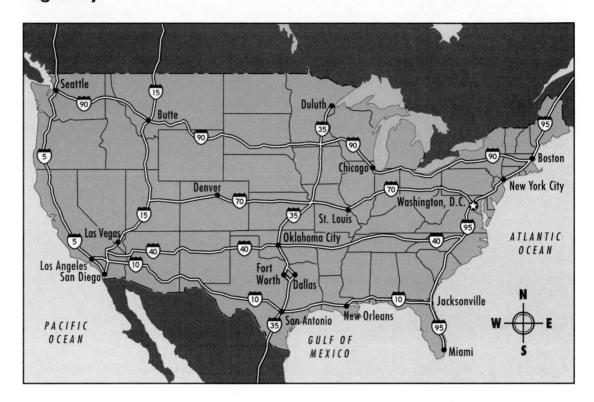

➤ How do I get from **New Orleans, Louisiana,** to **San Antonio, Texas?**

● Take **Interstate** _____ **west.**

Check Up

Use competencies 4 and 5. Use the map and the dialog above to ask for and give directions.

FROM	TO
1. Miami, Florida	Washington, D.C.
2. Los Angeles, California	Las Vegas, Nevada

Listening Transcript

Unit 1

Listening (Page 6)
Exercise A.
Look and listen. Who does Lucy introduce to Duc? Circle the answer for each conversation.

1. A: Hi, Duc. How are you?
   B: Hi, Lucy. Fine, thanks. How are you doing?
   A: Fine. I want you to meet my mother, Mrs. Blanco.
   B: Hi, Mrs. Blanco. It's nice to meet you.
   C: Nice to meet you, too, Duc. I've heard a lot about you.
2. A: I'd like you to meet my brother Manu. He's here visiting from the Philippines. Manu, this is Duc.
   B: Hello. Nice to meet you, Manu.
   C: It's nice to meet you, too.
   B: Are you staying long?
   C: About two more weeks, I think.
   B: Two weeks? Good. Maybe we can all do something together before you leave.
3. A: Duc, I'd like you to meet my cousin Rachel.
   B: Hi, Rachel. I didn't know Lucy had a cousin in town. Do you live here?
   C: Yes. I live with my parents.
   B: Well, it's very nice to meet you. What are you two doing today?
   A: We're going to the post office. Do you want to come?
   B: To the post office? Sure. I'll walk there with you.
4. A: Duc, have you met John Mantu?
   B: No, I haven't.
   A: John's my uncle. He's visiting from New York.
   B: Oh, Lucy's uncle. Nice to meet you.
   C: I'm sorry. What was your name again?
   B: It's Duc, spelled D-U-C.
   C: Oh, Duc. Nice to meet you, too.

Exercise B.
Who's getting a driver's license? Look, listen, and circle the letter of the picture.

A: May I help you?
B: Yes. I want to apply for a driver's license.

A: OK. Last name, please.
B: Thin. T-H-I-N.
A: T-H-I-N. And your first name?
B: Sang Qun. S-A-N-G Q-U-N.
A: Your address?
B: 2214 North Park Road. Miami, Florida 33153.
A: Birth date?
B: April 12, 1968.
A: Eye color?
B: Brown.
A: Sex . . . male. Your height?
B: Five feet three inches.
A: Weight?
B: 135.
A: Hair . . . black. Where were you born?
B: Pusan.
A: Where?
B: Pusan, Korea.
A: How do you spell Pusan?
B: P-U-S-A-N.
A: And your phone?
B: Area code 305–555–1831.
A: Could you repeat that?
B: 305–555–1831.
A: Thanks.

Listen again. Complete the driver's license application for San Qun Thin.
[Play the tape or read the manuscript of Exercise B aloud again.]

Unit 2

Listening (Page 20)
Exercise A.
Some people are at the post office.
Look and listen. Circle the kind of mail in column A.

1. A: May I help you?
   B: I want to send this letter to New York City.
   A: First class?
   B: Is that the fastest way?
   A: Yes. It takes about three days.
   B: How much will it cost to send it first class?
   A: 55¢.
   B: Oh good. I've got 55¢ in exact change. Here you go.

2. A: I'd like to send this package to Chile.
   B: Do you want insurance?
   A: I don't know. Do you think I should have it insured?
   B: Well, it's up to you. It depends on the value of the contents.
   A: It's about $150.
   B: Then it's probably a good idea to insure it. It's only $2.50.
   A: $2.50's not bad. I'll insure it.
3. A: May I help you?
   B: Yes. I want to send these books and magazines to San Diego.
   A: You can send books and magazines fourth class. It's cheaper that way.
   B: OK. I'll send the package fourth class then.
   A: The amount due is $5.02.
   B: $5.02 total? Thanks.

Listen again. Write the amount in column B. [Play the tape or read the manuscript of Exercise A aloud again.]

Exercise B.
Some people are at the bank. Look and listen. Circle the answer in column A.
1. A: I'd like to make a deposit.
   B: Is that a deposit to your checking account?
   A: No. To my savings account.
   B: And the amount?
   A: $212.
   B: OK. $212 deposited into your savings account.
2. A: May I help you?
   B: Yes. I want to make a deposit to my checking account.
   A: You need to fill out a deposit form.
   B: OK.
   A: Do you want cash returned?
   B: No. I want to deposit it all to checking: $416.25.
   A: OK. A deposit of $416.25.
3. A: Can I make a withdrawal? I forgot my card.
   B: I'll need to see two forms of identification.
   A: Here's my driver's license. And is a passport OK?
   B: Sure. Will the withdrawal be from your checking or savings account?
   A: Savings. It's for $75.00.

B: $20.00, $40.00, $60.00, $70.00, $75.00.
A: Thanks.
B: Thank you. Have a nice day.

Listen again. Write the amount in column B. [Play the tape or read the manuscript of Exercise B aloud again.]

Exercise C.
Look and listen. Write the information about bank savings plans.
1. A: City Savings. How may I help you?
   B: I want some information about your savings plan.
   A: All right. The minimum deposit required is $100.
   B: Is there a service charge?
   A: No. And we pay an interest rate of 5%.
   B: 5%? And a $100 minimum deposit?
   A: That's right.
   B: OK. Thank you.
2. A: Hello. Town Bank. May I help you?
   B: Yes. What's the interest rate on your savings accounts?
   A: It's 4%.
   B: Is there a minimum deposit?
   A: Yes. The minimum is $50.
   B: So you require a $50 deposit, and the interest rate is 4%. Is there a service charge?
   A: No. We have no service charge.
   B: Thanks very much.
3. A: This is National Savings. May I help you?
   B: Yes. I need some information about your savings accounts.
   A: OK. What information do you need?
   B: Well, first, what's the interest rate?
   A: The interest rate's 6%.
   B: 6%. That's good. Is there a minimum deposit?
   A: Yes. The minimum is $500.
   B: Is there a service charge?
   A: Yes. If your balance is under $1,000, there's a monthly service charge of $2.
   B: Let me see if I've got this. The interest rate is 6% and the minimum deposit is $500.
   A: That's right. And the monthly service charge is $2 if the balance is under $1,000.
   B: OK. Thanks very much.

Check Your Competency (Page 29)
Exercise C.
Use competency 3. Look and listen.
Write the amount due.

1. A: I'd like to send this letter to California.
   B: First class?
   A: Yes.
   B: You need one 32¢ stamp to mail it.
   A: Good. Let me see if I've got the exact change. Here you are—32¢.
2. A: I want to buy a money order.
   B: For how much?
   A: $100.00. Is there a fee?
   B: Yes. It's $1.00.
   A: So I owe you $101.00?
   B: Right.
3. A: Can I insure this package?
   B: Yes. What's its value?
   A: $150.00.
   B: The insurance on $150.00 is $2.50.
   A: Let's see . . . $2.50. OK. I'll insure it.
4. A: I want to send this letter to China.
   B: By air mail?
   A: Yes, air mail.
   B: That'll be 95¢.
   A: OK, here you go. 95¢.

Unit 3

Listening (Page 34)
Exercise A.
Listen and circle the answers.

Pablo: Hey, everybody! Guess what! I just became a citizen!

Ana: Really, Pablo? That's fantastic.

Chen: Yeah, that's great!

Ana: When did you find out?

Pablo: I just got the letter telling me about it today.

Chen: Was it hard to do, Pablo?

Pablo: Yes, Chen, it was pretty hard. After I came here, I had to become a permanent resident. That was a lot of work.

Ana: Then what?

Pablo: Well, then I had to wait for two more years. Then I applied for citizenship. I filled out an application form. Then I had to turn in some photographs.

Ana: And then?

Pablo: Then I had to pay a fee. After I paid the fee, I had to wait a long time for my interview. Then I had to wait for the results.

Chen: Well, congratulations, Pablo.

Pablo: Thanks. Are either of you thinking about becoming citizens? Ana?

Ana: Well, I'm a permanent resident, but I don't want to become a citizen. I don't want to lose my present nationality.

Chen: How come?

Ana: If I become a U.S. citizen, I'll have to give up my Spanish citizenship. I'd like to be able to return to Spain some day.

Pablo: Good point, Ana. If you want to return to Spain, you probably shouldn't become a citizen. For me it's different. I escaped from Cuba, so I can't go back. Chen, what about you? Are you going to become a citizen?

Chen: Well, I can go back to China if I want to, but I think I'd rather stay here. I really like the U.S. In fact, I'm applying for permanent residency right now.

Pablo: Good luck.

Chen: Thanks.

What are the people's reasons? Listen again and match. Write the letter. *[Play the tape or read the manuscript of Exercise A aloud again.]*

Listen again. Number Pablo's steps in order from 1 to 7. *[Play the tape or read the manuscript of Exercise A aloud again.]*

Unit 4

Listening (Page 48)
Exercise A.
Where did the people grow up? Look, listen, and number the pictures.

1. A: Where did you grow up?
   B: I grew up in a beautiful place in the mountains.
   A: What was it like?
   B: It was peaceful and quiet. My house was near a lake.

A: Really? Did you swim in the lake much?

B: No. The water was too cold. But we hiked in the mountains.

A: It sounds wonderful.

2. A: Did you grow up in the city?

B: Yes, I did. We moved to a big city when I was only two years old. I lived there all my life.

A: Do you like city life?

B: Yes, I do. There are exciting things to see and do. It's never boring.

A: It sounds like you love living in the city.

B: I do. That's why I live in New York now.

3. A: Have you ever been to the ocean before?

B: Oh, sure. In fact, I grew up on the coast.

A: Where?

B: I lived with my grandparents. They had a small house on the southeast coast of Korea.

Exercise B.

Look and listen. Dora, Truc, and Benito are talking. They're telling the class about their native countries. Circle the places where they are from.

1. My name is Dora. I'm from Ecuador. My father got a job in the U.S., and we all moved here with him. At first I felt scared. I wanted to go back to Ecuador. Then I started school. My English improved. I made new friends at school. I like going to school here now. I'm not scared or lonely anymore.

2. I'm Truc. I grew up in Vietnam. It was hard to live there because of the fighting. We lost our business. We were lucky to come to the U.S. to start over. We felt very hopeful when we came. Now we have our own shop. Things are going well. Next year we'll probably open another shop.

3. I'm Benito. I'm from Mexico. I have a large family in the U.S. I came to the U.S. to be with them. I liked it here right away. I felt very comfortable when I came. Parts of the Southwest are a lot like my home in Mexico. Right now I work in a hospital. I'd like to become a nurse some day.

Listen again. Circle how they felt when they arrived in the U.S. *[Play the tape or read the manuscript of Exercise B aloud again.]*

Listen again. What are they doing now? Complete the sentences. Write the letter.

[Play the tape or read the manuscript of Exercise B aloud again.]

Unit 5

Listening (Page 62)
Exercise A.
Listen to the cooking show. It's about making an omelet. Circle the ingredients.

Hello, and welcome to Ralph's Kitchen. Today I'd like to talk about omelets. Omelets are made with eggs, and they're easy to cook. They're excellent for breakfast, but they're also delicious for lunch and dinner. There are many kinds of omelets you can make, but today I'll be preparing a cheese omelet. To make a cheese omelet, you need two eggs, cheese, some milk, and some water.

Now we're ready to start. First grate about two ounces of cheese. Put two eggs in a bowl and stir them lightly with a fork. Then add two tablespoons of milk and one tablespoon of water to the eggs. Now you're ready to cook the omelet. Slowly put the egg mixture into the pan. Cook it on low heat for about five minutes. After that, put the cheese on top of the eggs and fold the omelet in half. Finally, cover the pan, turn off the heat, and wait three or four minutes. The omelet should be hot enough to melt the cheese.

Now your omelet is ready. Use a spatula to slide it onto your plate. Doesn't that smell good? Enjoy!

Listen again. Number the directions from 1 to 5. *[Play the tape or read the manuscript of Exercise A aloud again.]*

Exercise B.
Look and listen. Write what's on sale in column A.

1. Come to Food Fair where you can find all your favorite foods at great prices. This week we have a special on American cheese—perfect for topping hamburgers. Food Fair's American cheese is only $2.19 a package. What a bargain! And while you're in the dairy section, be sure to pick up some cold, fresh milk on sale at 79 cents a half-gallon.

And that's not all. Food Fair brand butter is on sale for 99 cents a pound. At Food Fair the bargains never stop!

2. For the best buys in groceries, shop Freshway! Freshway has specials every week. This week our produce section has a special on Idaho russet potatoes at 32 cents a pound. Buy now while the supply lasts.

While you're in the produce section, take a look at Freshway's special of the week. Sweet, juicy Florida oranges are just 89 cents a pound. That's a bargain you shouldn't miss!

And in our meat market, Freshway is happy to offer chicken at only 79 cents a pound. Buy now! You won't want to miss the specials at Freshway.

Listen again. Write the prices in column B. *[Play the tape or read the manuscript of Exercise B aloud again.]*

Check Your Competency (Page 71)
Exercise B.
Use competency 2. Look and listen. What's on sale? Write the prices.

1. Shoppers! Come to Big's Market, where every day is a special day and a day of specials! This week in our produce section, we have mushrooms for only 99 cents a pound. With bargains like this, you can't afford to shop anywhere else.

2. What's on sale at William's this week? We have juicy red onions at only 49 cents a pound. That's right, 49 cents a pound. All our produce is marked well below our competitors' prices. So shop at William's Grocery for the best in produce and the best prices, too.

3. This week only at Super Save Foods, you can buy tomato sauce in 10-ounce cans for only 69 cents a can. Offer available while supplies last, and at 69 cents a can, this bargain will go fast. So come in to take advantage of this special buy and all the other great prices at Super Save. Super Save Foods. Our name says it all!

Unit 6

Listening (Page 76)
Exercise A.
Dean and Sue are shopping for a sweater for their mother. Look, listen, and write the price in column A.

1. A: How do you like this sweater?
   B: Well, Mom likes white a lot. It's her favorite color.
   A: Hmmm, . . . and it's in our price range— $19.99.
   B: $19.99? You're right. It's not too expensive.
   A: It looks pretty nice. And it's probably machine washable.
   B: Yes. The label says *machine wash.* Do you think we should buy it?
   A: Maybe. Let's keep looking. We might see something we like better.

2. A: Oh, I like this sweater!
   B: Yeah, it's really pretty. How much is it?
   A: It's on sale for only $24.99.
   B: $24.99? Gee, that's a pretty good price.
   A: What's the care label say? Is it machine washable?
   B: Let me look. . . . No. You have to hand wash it.
   A: Hmmm. That's a lot of work. I don't know. . . .
   B: Do you think Mom would like it?
   A: Probably. But she wouldn't want to hand wash it.
   B: You're right. The other sweater is really Mom's favorite color.
   A: Yeah. Maybe we should get the white one. It's her favorite color, and she can machine wash it.
   B: Yes. Let's get her the first one. We could get her some flowers, too.
   A: That's a great idea.

Listen again. How should you wash the sweater? Write *machine wash* or *hand wash* in column B. *[Play the tape or read the manuscript of Exercise A aloud again.]*

Listen again. Why did they buy the white sweater? Circle the reasons. *[Play the tape or read the manuscript of Exercise A aloud again.]*

Exercise B.
Look. listen, and complete the return forms.

1. A: I'd like to return these towels.
   B: Do you have the receipt?
   A: Yes. Here it is.
   B: What's the reason for the return?
   A: They're the wrong color.
   B: Would you like another color towel?
   A: No. I just want a refund.
   B: All right. Please complete this form to get your refund.
   A: OK. Thank you.
2. A: This shirt is the wrong size. I want to exchange it for a larger one.
   B: Do you have the receipt?
   A: No, I don't, but the shirt still has the tags on it.
   B: Great. I can exchange it for you. Please complete this form. Then you can look for the shirt in your size.
   A: OK. Thanks very much.

Unit 7

Listening (Page 90)
Exercise A.
Three people are calling about places to rent. Look and listen. Number the homes.

1. A: Hello.
   B: Hello. I'm calling about the one-bedroom apartment for rent. Is it still available?
   A: Yes, that apartment is still for rent.
   B: And the rent is $315?
   A: Hmmm, . . . yes. $315. We also ask for one month's rent—$315—as a deposit.
   B: OK. Well, are the utilities included?
   A: We pay water.
   B: Hmmm, water is included. What else can you tell me about the apartment?
   A: Well, there's a stove and a refrigerator. But there's no washer or dryer.
   B: That's OK with me. Oh yes, I have a cat. Are pets a problem?

   A: I'm sorry. We don't allow pets.
   B: Oh, too bad. Well, thanks anyway.
2. A: Greenway Mobile Home Park.
   B: Hello. I understand you have a mobile home for rent.
   A: Yes, we do.
   B: Could you tell me about the rent and deposit?
   A: Certainly. The rent is $500 per month and the deposit is $250.
   B: $500 per month. And the deposit is . . . ?
   A: $250.
   B: Are the utilities paid?
   A: Yes. The mobile home park pays gas, electricity, and water.
   B: Wonderful! Does the home come with any appliances?
   A: Sure. There's a stove and a refrigerator in the kitchen. There's also a washer and dryer.
   B: Great! Stove, refrigerator, and washer and dryer. I'm very interested.
   A: Did I tell you that we don't allow pets?
   B: That's all right. I don't have any.
3. A: World Realty. May I help you?
   B: Yes. I'm calling about a two-bedroom house I saw for rent on Dewey Avenue. How much is the rent?
   A: Let's see. . . . The rent on that house is $450 a month.
   B: $450 a month seems reasonable. How much is the deposit?
   A: We ask for one month's rent as a deposit.
   B: One month's rent . . . $450. I see. What else can you tell me?
   A: Well, you have to pay all the utilities yourself. But we do allow pets.
   B: Oh, pets are OK. That's good. I have a cat. But no utilities are paid? Not even water?
   A: No, I'm sorry.
   B: Well, are there any appliances?
   A: There's a stove and a refrigerator.
   B: Is there a washer and dryer?
   A: No, I'm afraid not.
   B: Well, thanks anyway. I guess I'm not interested.

Listen again. Write the rent and the deposit. *[Play the tape or read the manuscript of Exercise A aloud again.]*

Listen again. Which utilities are included? Are pets allowed? *[Play the tape or read the manuscript of Exercise A aloud again.]*

Unit 8

Listening (Page 104)
Exercise A.
Look and listen. Three people are seeing doctors. Circle the doctors they're seeing in column A.

1. A: Hello, Ms. Quintana.
   B: Hello, Dr. Evans.
   A: Let's see. . . . Your last pregnancy check-up was two weeks ago and everything was fine. How are you doing now?
   B: Well, I think the baby is doing fine, but I don't feel very well.
   A: What's the matter?
   B: I think I have a cold.
   A: No problems with the pregnancy though?
   B: No. Everything seems fine there.
   A: OK. Let's talk about this cold first, and then we'll do a regular pregnancy check-up.
   B: OK. Well, I have a cough and my head hurts.
   A: Hmmm . . . it sounds like you have a cold.
   B: Can I take some aspirin for the headache?
   A: No. I don't want you to take any aspirin during your pregnancy. I'll write down some cough medicine you can take, though.
   B: OK. Thanks, Dr. Evans.

2. A: Good morning, Mr. Park. What brings you here today?
   B: Good morning, Dr. Tena. I've been having some problems with my eyes lately.
   A: Do you have trouble seeing?
   B: Sometimes. It's hard to read the board at school.
   A: Well, maybe you need glasses. You need to have an eye test to find out.
   B: OK.
   A: Have a seat over here and we can begin the eye test.

3. A: Good afternoon, Mr. McMillan. I'm Dr. Anaya. And this must be Matthew. Hi there, Matthew.
   C: Hi, doctor.

B: Nice to meet you, Dr. Anaya. I'm glad you could see us. My friend Ms. Collier says you're a very good pediatrician.
A: Well, I'm glad I could fit you in. Now what seems to be the matter? Doesn't Matthew feel well?
B: No. He has an earache in both ears. It started two days ago.
A: Hmmm. . . . He has a slight fever, too. His temperature is 99.5°. Has he had a stomachache?
B: No, no stomachache. Just an earache and a fever.
A: OK, let me take a look at his ears. I'm going to look in your ears. OK, Matthew?
C: OK.
A: Well, his ears are a little red. But I don't think it's serious. Do your ears hurt right now, Matthew?
C: Ummm . . . maybe a little bit.
A: OK. Well, Mr. McMillan, I'm going to give you a prescription for Matthew. His earache should go away two or three days after he starts taking this medicine.
B: All right. When do I give him the medicine?
A: Give it to him once a day after a meal. OK, Matthew. I hope you feel better. And, Mr. McMillan, feel free to call if his earache doesn't get better.
B: OK, Dr. Anaya. Thanks.

Listen again. What's the matter with the people? Circle the answer in column B.
[Play the tape or read the manuscript of Exercise A aloud again.]

Listen again. What do the doctors say to do? Circle the answer in column C. *[Play the tape or read the manuscript of Exercise A aloud again.]*

Check Your Competency (Page 113)
Exercise F.
Use competency 6. Look and listen. What does the doctor tell the patient? Circle the answers.

A: Hello, Mr. Wong.
B: Hello, Dr. Mendoza.

A: How do you feel?

B: Not very well. I have a cough and my head hurts.

A: Hmmm . . . do you have a stomachache, too?

B: No, I don't.

A: Well, it's probably not the flu then. You probably just have a bad cold.

B: What should I do?

A: Take some aspirin for your headache. And some cough medicine for your cough.

B: What kind of cough medicine should I take?

A: I can write down the name of a good one. If you take the aspirin and the cough medicine, you should feel better soon.

Unit 9

Listening (Page 118)
Exercise A.
Three people are at job interviews. Look and listen. Circle the jobs they want in column A.

1. A: Hello. My name is Sue Jung Ma. I'm applying for a job as electronics assembler.

   B: Have you ever worked as an electronics assembler before?

   A: Yes. I was an electronics assembler for six years at a company in Korea.

   B: Six years. Well, your experience as an electronics assembler makes you a very good person for this job. I need to talk to all the applicants, and then I'll call you later in the week.

   A: OK. Thank you very much.

2. A: Ms. Wu? I'm Manuel Domingo. I'm here to talk about a job with your company as a carpenter.

   B: Oh, yes. Nice to meet you, Manuel. Please sit down.

   A: Thank you.

   B: You wrote on your application that you have some experience as a carpenter.

   A: I do. I worked as a carpenter in Mexico. I also had a few jobs on construction projects here in the U.S.

   B: How long have you been a carpenter?

A: For five years. Three years in Mexico and two years here.

B: Well, Manuel, I think this may work out for both of us. When can you start?

A: I can start next week. Is that OK?

B: That's fine. Come in on Monday at 7 A.M.

A: OK. Thank you very much.

3. A: Hello. My name is Shelly Darrow. I want to apply for the housekeeper position.

   B: Oh, hello. Is it Shelly?

   A: Yes, Shelly Darrow.

   B: Nice to meet you. I'm Fatima Tajiri. I'm the housekeeping manager. Do you have experience as a housekeeper?

   A: No, I don't. But I learn quickly.

   B: Hmmm, . . . no experience. Well, that's OK. You seem very enthusiastic.

   A: I am. I really want this job. I have good references, too.

   B: OK, that's good. Let me go get the hotel manager to talk with you, Shelly. Please wait here.

   A: OK. Thank you.

Listen again. How much experience do they have? Circle the answer in column
B. *[Play the tape or read the manuscript of Exercise A aloud again.]*

Exercise B. It's Shelly's first day of work as a housekeeper. What does she have to do? Circle the instructions.

A: OK, Shelly, this is the first room on your schedule. First, you have to make the beds and vacuum the room.

B: Does it matter if I vacuum the room before I make the beds?

A: No. You can do either first.

B: Good. Then what?

A: Then empty the trash cans.

B: Where do I put the trash? Could you show me, please?

A: Yes. Empty the cans into this trash bin on the cart.

B: What do I do next?

A: In the bathroom clean the sink, the toilet, and the bathtub.

B: OK. Clean the sink, toilet, and tub. Anything else in the bathroom?

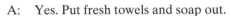

A: Yes. Put fresh towels and soap out.

B: OK. I think I can remember all that.

A: Good. If you need anything or have any questions, you should ask me.

B: All right, thanks.

Check Your Competency (Page 127)
Exercise C.
Use competency 5. Listen. It's Ernesto's first day as a custodian. What does Ernesto have to do? Circle the answers.

A: Hi, Mr. Ramos. I'm Ernesto, the new custodian. What do I have to do?

B: Well, hello, Ernesto. Nice to meet you. The first thing you need to do is vacuum the offices.

A: Vacuum the offices. OK. Where's the vacuum cleaner? Could you show me, please?

B: Yes, it's in this closet right here. Next empty all the trash cans.

A: Empty all the trash cans. OK.

B: Then please clean the bathrooms in the outer hall.

A: I'm sorry. Where are the bathrooms?

B: In the outer hall.

A: Oh, OK. Anything else?

B: That's all for now. We can go over your other duties later.

A: OK, thanks. I'll get right to work.

Unit 10

Listening (Page 132)
Exercise B.
Emily is asking a friend for directions to Dallas from Chicago. Listen. Mark the route on the map.

A: Hi, Emily. Are you all ready to go to Dallas?

B: Oh, hi, Yolanda. Yes, I guess so. I had my car tuned up and I checked everything on it myself this afternoon. I leave tomorrow morning. I'm not sure which route I'll take though. What highways do you usually take to go to Dallas?

A: Well . . . here, I'll show you a good route to take on this map. First I'd take Interstate 57 south to Interstate 70. Then I'd take Interstate 70 west to St. Louis. You could stay there tomorrow night.

B: 57 to 70? Yeah, that's the route I always take to St. Louis. Then what?

A: Well, the next day I'd take Interstate 55 south from St. Louis. Interstate 55 takes you to Memphis. I'd stay there a night, too. You don't want to drive too much in one day.

B: Good idea. Is 55 a pretty nice route?

A: I think so. It's better to take Interstate 55 than to take a smaller highway. I stay on the main roads when I travel.

B: That sounds like a good idea. I guess you take Interstate 40 west from Memphis, then, right?

A: Right. Interstate 40 takes you to Little Rock. Then you can take Interstate 30 all the way down to Dallas.

B: Oh, you have to get on Interstate 30 in Little Rock? Can't you stay on 40?

A: No. Interstate 40 takes you up to Oklahoma City, see?

B: Oh, yes, I see. Interstate 40 goes northwest from Little Rock. So let me see . . . . Oh yeah, here's Interstate 30 from Little Rock. Do you think I can drive from Memphis to Little Rock to Dallas in one day?

A: Yeah. It's a long day's trip, but you should be able to make it. Well, Emily, have a safe trip. And good luck in your new job.

B: Thanks. It should be an interesting trip. And I'm excited about my new job. I'll miss you and your family, though. You've been wonderful neighbors, Yolanda.

A: We'll miss you, too, Emily. Bye.

B: So long.